I0052480

Position Perspective Opportunities Probability Vulnerabilities Rewards Momentum Situations Mistakes

IX

孫子兵法

Sun Tzu's
Art of War
Playbook
Volume 9 of 9:
Vulnerabilities

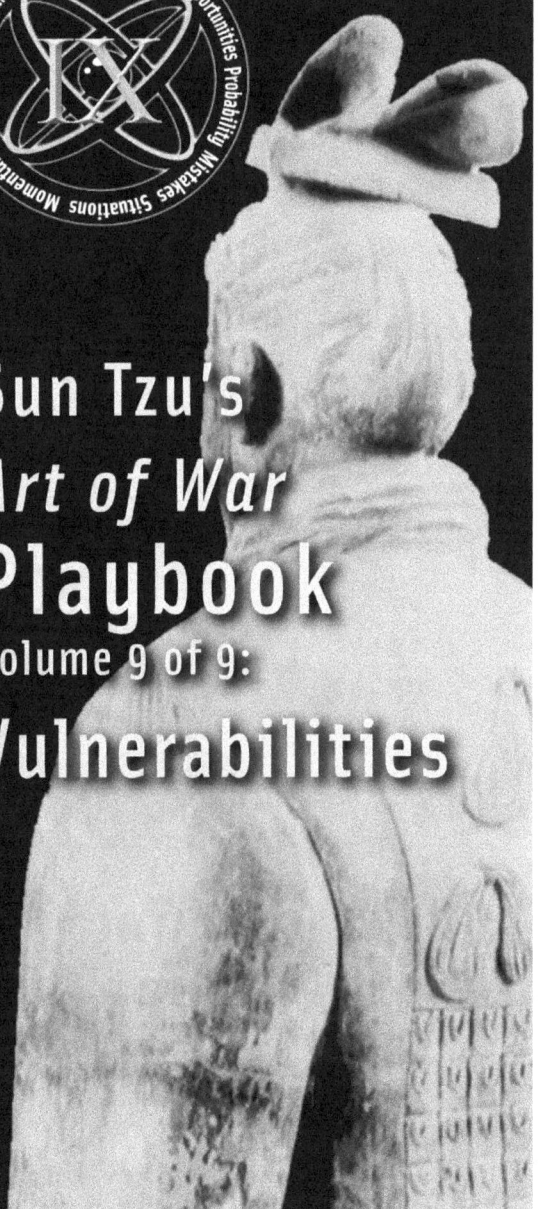

Gary
Gagliardi

Sun Tzu's Art of War

Playbook

Volume Nine:
Vulnerabilities

by Gary Gagliardi
The Science of Strategy Institute
Clearbridge Publishing

Published by
Science of Strategy Institute, Clearbridge Publishing
       suntzus.com   scienceofstrategy.org

First Print Edition
Library of Congress Control Number: 2014909969
Also sold as an ebook under the title Sun Tzu's Warrior Playbook
Copyright 2010, 2011, 2012, 2013, 2014 Gary Gagliardi
ISBN 978-1-929194-84-1 (13-digit) 1-929194-84-6 (10-digit)

All rights reserved. No part of this book may be reproduced or transmitted in any part or by
any means, electronic or mechanical, including photocopying, recording, or by any information storage
and retrieval system, without the written permission of the Publisher, except where
permitted by law.

Registered with Department of Copyrights, Library of Congress.

Originally published as a series of articles on the Science of Strategy Website, scienceofstratregy.org. and
later as an ebook on various sites.

PO Box 33772, Seattle, WA 98133
Phone: (206)542-8947 Fax: (206)546-9756
beckyw@clearbridge.com
garyg@scienceofstrategy.org

Manufactured in the United States of America.
Interior and cover graphic design by Dana and Jeff Wincapaw.
Original Chinese calligraphy by Tsai Yung, Green Dragon Arts, www.greendragonarts.com.

Publisher's Cataloging-in-Publication Data
Sun-tzu, 6th cent. B.C.
Strategy , positioning, success, probability
      [Sun-tzu ping fa, English]
      Art of War Playbook / Sun Tzu and Gary Gagliardi.
      p.197 cm. 23
      Includes introduction to basic competitive philosophy of Sun Tzu

Clearbridge Publishing's books may be purchased for business, for any promotional use,
or for special sales.

Contents

Playbook Overview

Note: This overview is provided for those who have not read the previous volume of Sun Tzu's Art of War Playbook. *It provides an brief overview of the work in general and the general concepts framing the first volume.*

Sun Tzu's **The Art of War** is less a "book" in the modern Western sense than it is an outline for a course of study. Like Euclid's Geometry, simply reading the work teaches us very little. Sun Tzu wrote in in a tradition that expected each line and stanza to be studied in the context of previous statements to build up the foundation for understanding later statements.

To make this work easier for today's readers to understand, we developed the **Strategy Playbook**, the Science of Strategy Institute (SOSI) guidebook to explaining Sun Tzu's strategy in the more familiar format of a series of explanations with examples. These lessons are framed in the context of modern competition rather than ancient military warfare.

This Playbook is the culmination of over a decade of work breaking down Sun Tzu's principles into a series of step-by-step practical articles by the Institute's multiple award-winning author and founder, Gary Gagliardi. The original *Art of War* was written for military generals who understood the philosophical concepts of ancient China, which in itself is a practical hurdle that most modern readers cannot clear. Our *Art of War Playbook* is written for today's reader. It puts Sun Tzu's ideas into everyday, practical language.

The Playbook defines a new science of strategic competition aimed at today's challenges. This science of competition is designed as the complementary opposite of the management science that is taught in most business schools. This science starts, as Sun Tzu did himself, by defining a better, more complete vocabulary for discussing competitive situations. It connects the timeless ideas of Sun Tzu to today's latest thinking in business, mathematics, and psychology.

The entire Playbook consists of two hundred and thirty articles describing over two-thousand interconnected key methods. These articles are organized into nine different areas of strategic skill from understanding positioning to defending vulnerabilities. All together this makes up over a thousand pages of material.

Playbook Access

The Playbook's most up-to-date version is available as separate articles on our website. Live links make it easy to access the connections between various articles and concepts. If you become a SOSI Member, you can access any Playbook article at any time and access their links.

However, at the request of our customers, we also offer these articles as a series of nine eBooks. Each of the nine sections of the entire Playbook makes up a separate eBook, Playbook Parts One Through Nine. These parts flow logically through the Progress Cycle of listen-aim-move-claim (see illustration). Because of the dynamic nature of the on-line version, these eBooks are not going to be as current as the on-line version. You can see a outline of current Playbook articles here and, generally, the eBook version will contain most of the same material in the same order.

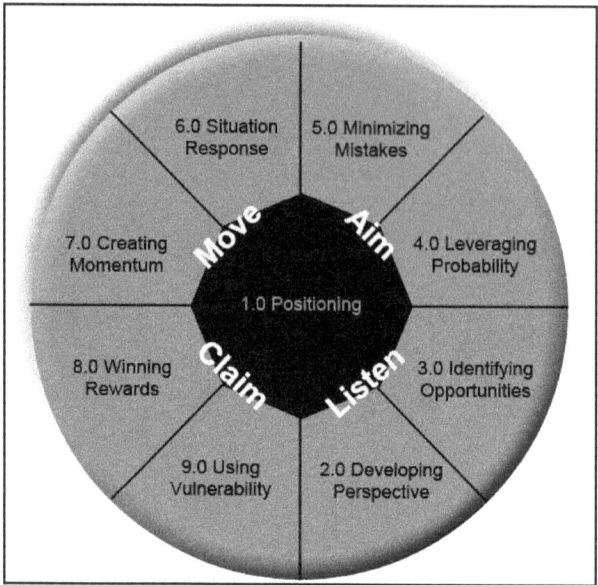

Nine categories of strategic skills define cycle that advances our positions:

1. Comparing Positions,

2. Developing Perspective,

3. Identifying Opportunities,

4. Leveraging Probability,

5. Minimizing Mistakes,

6. Responding To Situations,

7. Creating Momentum,

8. Winning Rewards, And

9. Defending Vulnerabilities.

Playbook Structure and Design

These articles are written in standard format including 1) the general principle, 2) the situation, 3) the opportunity, 4) the list of specific Art of War key methods breaking down the general principle into a series of actions, and 5) an illustration of the application of each of those key methods to a specific competitive situation. Key methods are written generically to apply to every competitive arena (business, personal life, career, sports, relationships, etc.) with each specific illustrations drawn from one of these areas.

A number identifies where each article appears in Playbook Structure. For example, the article 2.1.3 Strategic Deception is the third article in the first section of the second book in the nine volumes of the Strategy Playbook. In our on-line version, these links are live, clicking on them brings you to the article itself. We provide them because the interconnection of concepts is important in learning Sun Tzu's system.

Playbook Training

Training in Sun Tzu's warrior skills does not entail memorizing all these principles. Instead, these concepts are used to develop exercises and tools that allow trainees to put this ideas in practice. While each rule is useful, the heart of Sun Tzu system is the methods that connect all the principles together. Training in these principles is designed to develop a gut instinct for how Sun Tzu's strategy is used in different situations to produce success. Principles are interlinked because they describe a comprehensive conceptual mental model. Warrior Class training puts trainees in a situation where they must constantly make decisions, rewarding them for making decisions consist with winning productively instead of destructively.

About Positions

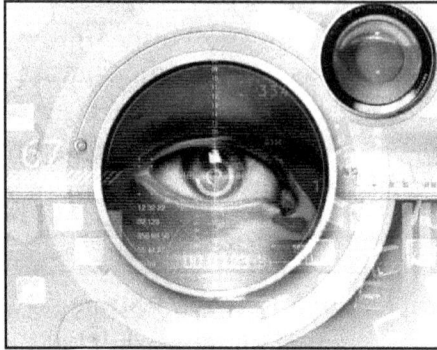

This first volume of Sun Tzu's Playbook focuses on teaching us the nature of strategic positions. "Position awareness" gives you a framework for understanding your strategic situation relative to the conditions around you. It enables you to see your position as part of a larger environment constructed of other positions and the raw elements that create positions. Master Sun Tzu's system of comparing positions, you can understand which aspect of your position are secure and which are the most dynamic and likely to change.

Traditional strategy defines a "position" as a comparison of situations. Game theory defines is as the current decision point that is arrive at as the sum or result of all previous decisions, both yours and those of others. Sun Tzu's methods of positioning awareness are different. They force you to see yourself in the eyes of others. Using these techniques, you broaden your perspective by gathering a range of viewpoints. In a limited sense, the scope of your position defines your area of control within your larger environment. In traditional strategy, five elements--mission, climate, ground, command, and methods--define the dimensions in which competitors can be compared.

Competition as Comparison

Sun Tzu saw that success is based on comparisons. This comparison must take place whenever a choice is made. For Sun Tzu, competition means a comparison of alternative choices or "positions". Battles are won by positioning before they are fought. These positions provide choices for everyone involved. Good positions discourage others from attacking you and invite them to support you. Sun Tzu's system teaches us how to systematically build up our positions to win success in the easiest way possible.

Competing positions are compared on the basis many elements, both objective and subjective. Sun Tzu's strategy is to identify these points of comparison and to understand how to leverage them. Learning Sun Tzu's strategy requires learning the details of how positions are compared and advanced. Sun Tzu taught that fighting to "sort things out" is a foolish way to find learn the strengths and weaknesses of a position. Conflict to tear down opposing positions is the most costly way to win competitive comparisons.

Today's More Competitive World

In the complex, chaotic world of today, we can easily get trapped into destructive rather than productive situations. Even our smallest decisions can have huge impact on our future. The problem is that we are trained for yesterday's world of workers, not today's world of warriors. We are trained in the linear thinking of planning in predictable, hierarchical world. This thinking applies less and less to today's networked, more competitive world.

Following a plan is the worker's skill of working in pre-defined functions in an internal, stable, controlled environment. The competitive strategy of Sun Tzu is the warrior's skill of making good decisions about conditions in complex, fast-changing, competitive environments. Sun Tzu's strategic system teaches us to adapt to the unexpected events that are becoming more and more common in our lives. We live in a world where fewer and fewer key events are planned. Navigating our new world of external challenges requires a different set of skills.

Most of us make our decisions without any understanding of competition. The result is that most of us lose as many battles as we win, never making consistent progress. Events buffet us, turning us in one direction and then the other. Too often, we end up repeating our past patterns of mistakes.

The Science of Strategy Institute teaches you the warrior's skills of adaptive response. There are many organizations that teach planning and organization. The Institute is one of the few places in the world you can get learn competitive thinking, and the only place in the world, with a comprehensive Playbook.

Seeing Situations Differently

Sun Tzu taught that a warrior's decision-making was a matter of reflex. As we develop our strategic decision-making skills, the critical conditions in situations simply "pop" out at us. This isn't magic. The latest research on how decisions are made tells us a lot about why Sun Tzu's principles work. It comes from using patterns to retrain our mind to see conditions differently. The study of successful response arose from military confrontations, where every battle clearly demonstrated how hard it is to predict events in the real world. Sun Tzu saw that winners were always those who knew how to respond appropriately to the dynamic nature of their situation.

Sun Tzu's principles provides a complete model for the key knowledge for understanding conditions in complex dynamic environments. This model "files" each piece of data into the appropriate place in the big picture. As the picture of your situation fills in, you can identify the opportunities hidden within your situation.

Making Decisions about Conditions

Instead of focusing on a series of planned steps, Sun Tzu's principles are about making decisions regarding conditions. It concerns itself with: 1) identifying the relative strengths and weaknesses of competitive positions, 2) advancing positions leveraging opportunities, and 3) the types of responses to specific challenges that work the most frequently. Using Sun Tzu's principles, we call these three areas position awareness , opportunity development , and situation response . Each area that we master broadens your capabilities.

- Position awareness trains us to recognize that competitive situations are defined by the relationship among alternative positions. Developing this perspective never ends. It deepens throughout our lives.
- Opportunity development explores the ground, testing our perceptions. Only testing the edges of perspective through action can we know what is true.
- S ituation response trains us to recognize the key characteristics of the immediate situation and to respond appropriately. Only by practice, can we learn to trust the viewpoint we have developed.

Success in competitive environments comes from making better decisions every day. Sharp strategic reflexes flow from a clear understanding of where and when you use which competitive tools methods.

The Key Viewpoints

As an individual, you have a unique and valuable viewpoint, but every viewpoint is inherently limited by its own position. The result is that people cannot get a useful perspective on their own situations and surrounding opportunities. The first formula of positioning awareness involve learning what information is relevant. The most advanced techniques teach how to gather that information and put it into a bigger picture.

Most people see their current situations as the sum of their past successes and failures. Too often people dwell on their mistakes while simultaneously sitting on their laurels. Sun Tzu's strategy forces you to see your position differently. How you arrived at your current position doesn't matter. Your position is what it is. It is shaped by history but history is not destiny.

In this framework, the only thing that matters is where you are going and how you are going to get there. As you begin to develop your strategic reflexes, you start to think more and more about how to secure your current position and advance it.

Seeing the Big Picture

Most people see all the details of their lives, but they cannot see what those detail mean in terms of the big picture. As you master position awareness, you don't see your life as a point but as a path. You see your position in terms of what is changing and what resources are available. You are more aware of your ability to make decisions and your skills in working with others.

Most importantly, this strategic system forces you to get in touch with your core set of goals and values.

Untrained people usually see their life in terms of absolutes: successes and failures, good luck and bad, weakness and strength. As you begin to master position awareness, you begin to see all comparisons of strength and weakness are temporary and relative. A position is not strong or weak in itself. Its strength or weakness depends on how it compares or "fits" with surrounding positions. Weakness and strength are not what a position is, but how you use it.

The Power of Perspective

Positional awareness gives you the specialized vocabulary you need to understanding how situations develop. Mastering this vocabulary, you begin to see the leverage points connecting past and future. You replace vague conceptions of "strength," "momentum," and "innovation" with much more pragmatic definitions that you can actually use on a day to day basis.

Mastering position awareness also changes your relationships with other people. It teaches you a different way of judging truth and character. This methods allow you to spot self-deception and dishonest in others. It also allows you to understand how you can best work with others to compensate for your different weaknesses.

Once you develop a good perspective of position, it naturally leads you to want to learn more about how you can improve you position through the various aspects of opportunity development covered in the subsequent parts of the Strategy Playbook.

Seeing the Invisible

The "Nazca lines" are giant drawings etched across thirty miles of desert on Peru's southern coast. The patterns are only visible at a distance of hundreds of feet in the air. Below that, they look like strange paths or roads to nowhere. Just as we cannot see these lines without the proper perspective, people who master Sun Tzu's methods can <u>suddenly recognize situations</u> that were invisible to them before. Unless we have the right perspective, we cannot compare situations and positions successfully. The most recent scientific research explains why people cannot see these patterns for comparison without developing the network framework of adaptive thinking.[1]

Seeing Patterns

We can imagine patterns in chaotic situations, but seeing real pattern is the difference between success and failure. In our seminars, we demonstrate the power of seeing patterns in a number of exercises.

The <u>mental models</u> used by warrior give them "situation awareness." This situation awareness isn't just vague theory. Recent research shows that it can be measured in a variety of ways.[2] We now know that untrained people fall victim to a flow of confusing information because they don't know where its pieces fit. Those trained in Sun Tzu's mental models plug this stream of information quickly and easily into a bigger picture, transforming the skeleton's provided by Sun Tzu's system into a functioning awareness of your strategic position and its relation to other positions. Each piece of information has a place in that picture. As the information comes in, it fills in the picture, like pieces of a puzzle.

The ability to see the patterns in this bigger picture allows experts in strategy to see what is invisible to most people in a number of ways. They include:

- People trained in Art of War principles--<u>recognition-primed decision-making</u> --see patterns that others do not.
- Trained people can spot anomalies, things that should happen in the network of interactions but don't.
- Trained people are in touch with changes in the environment within appropriate time horizons.
- Trained people recognize complete patterns of interconnected elements under extreme time pressure.

Procedures Make Seeing Difficult

One of the most surprising discoveries from this research is that those who know procedures, that is, a linear view of events, alone have a ***more*** difficult time recognizing patterns than novices. An interesting study[3] examined the different recognition skills of three groups of people 1) experts, 2) novices, and 3) trainers who taught the standard procedures. The three groups were asked to pick out an expert from a group novices in a series of videos showing them performing a decision-making task, in this case, CPR. Experts were able to recognize the expert 90% of the time. Novices recognized the expert 50% of the time. The shocking fact was that trainers performed much worse that the novices, recognizing the expert only 30% of the time.

Why do those who know procedures fail to see what the experts usually see and even novices often see? Because, as research into <u>mental simulations</u> has shown, those with only a procedural model fit everything into that model and ignore elements that don't fit. In the above experiment, interviews with the trainers indicated that they assumed that the experts would always follow the procedural model. In real life, experts adapt to situations where unique conditions often trump procedure. Adapting to the situation rather than following set procedures is a central focus the form of strategy that the Institute teaches.

Missing Expected Elements

People trained to recognize the bigger picture beyond procedures also recognize when expected elements are missing from the picture. These anomalies or, what the cognition experts[4] describe as "negative cues" are invisible to novices *and* to those trained only in procedure. Without sense of the bigger pattern, people are focused too narrowly on the problem at hand. The "dog that didn't bark" from the Sherlock Holmes story, "Silver Blaze," is the most famous example of a negative cue. Only those working from a larger nonprocedural framework can expect certain things to happen and notice when they don't.

The ability to see what is missing also comes from the expectations generated by the mental model. Process-oriented models have the expectation of one step following another, but situation-recognition models create their expectations from signals in the environment. Research[5] into the time horizons of decision-makers shows that different time scales are at work. People at the highest level of organizations must look a year or two down the road, using strategic models that work in that timeframe, doing strategic planning. Decision-makers on the front-lines, however, have to react within minutes or even seconds to changes in their situation, working from their strategic reflexes. The biggest danger is that people get so wrapped up in a process that they lose contact with their environment.

Decisions Under Pressure

Extreme time pressure is what distinguishes front-line decision-making from strategic planners. One of the biggest discoveries in cognitive research[6] is that trained people do much better in seeing their situation instantly and making the correct decisions under time pressure. Researchers found virtually no difference between the decisions that experts made under time pressure when comparing them to decisions made without time pressure. That research also finds that those with less experience and training made dramatically worse decisions when they were put under time pressure.

The central argument for training our strategic reflexes is that our situation results, not from chance or luck, but from the instant decisions that that we all make every day. Our position is the sum of these decisions. If we cannot make the right decisions on the spot, when they are needed, our plans usually come to nothing. This is why we describe training people's strategic reflexes as helping them "do at first what most people only do at last."

The success people experience seeing what is invisible to others is dramatic. To learn more about how the strategic reflexes we teach differ from what can be planned, read about the contrast between planning and reflexes here . As our many members report, the success Sun Tzu's system makes possible is remarkable.

1 Chi, Glaser, & Farr, 1988, The Nature of Expertise, Erlbaum
2 Endsley & Garland, Analysis and Measurement of Situation Awareness
3 Klein & Klein, 1981, "Perceptual/Cognitive Analysis of proficient CPR Performance", Midwestern Psychological Association Meeting, Chicago.
4 Dr. David Noble, Evidence Based Research, Inc.In Gary Klein, Sources of Power, 1999
5 Jacobs & Jaques, 1991, "Executive Leadership".In Gal & Mangelsdofs (eds.), Handbook of Military Psychology, Wiley
6 Calder, Klein, Crandall,1988, "Time Pressure, Skill, and Move Quality in Chess". American Journal of Psychology, 101:481-493

About Vulnerabilities

After you have proven that your advanced position pays, you need to defend that position. Until you secure its safety, you have not finished advancing your position. New positions are fragile. Competitors are quick to copy successes. You must protect the key resources on which your new position depends. This is the topic of this final volume of Sun Tzu's Playbook.

Sun Tzu's principles concerning the vulnerabilities covered in this volume are ambiguous. They can be read as a guide to protecting a position or attacking it. To Sun Tzu, attacking and defending are two sides of the same process. You cannot do one without understanding the other.

In this volume, we look at these issues mostly from the point of view of defense, simply because so many other parts of Sun Tzu's methods focus on advancing a position. The perspective teaches you to recognize when you are vulnerable. It teaches you to prepare for the most common forms of attack. When you have a dominant position, you cannot leave openings through which opponents can undermine you. Most attacks are harmless if you respond appropriately, and that is why you must master this final formula.

The final line of defense is protecting yourself from direct attacks that are invited by your areas of vulnerability, the focus of this chapter. These vulnerabilities arise out of the fact that the climate is always changing, creating potential openings for rivals. We can categorize these types of vulnerabilities as *climate vulnerabilities* because they arise from changes in the environment. Those who might use these vulnerabilities against us are called *climate rivals.* We refer to the use of these vulnerabilities against us as *climate attacks.*

Success Is Always a Target

You must defend any new, successful position against competitors. Success invites competition. Success invites imitation. Success invites attack. All these principles factor in this fact of human nature.

Fortunately, it is easier to defend an established position than it is to build it. As long as you don't take your new position for granted, the techniques of defending a position are relatively easy. Defense is easier and more certain than advance.

Your first line of defense is pursuing opportunities that are easy to defend. This is the focus of Volume Four of the Playbook. Your second line of defense is responding to competitive situations correctly. This is the focus of Volume Six.

The Five Targets

The first principles discussed in this volume relate to defending the resources on which your current position depends. Sun Tzu teaches the positions depend on five resources: individual supports, short-term assets, logistical resources, long-term assets, and organizational relationships. There are five targets in a changing environment that competitors will target as vulnerabilities.

1. First, they will try to win away your supporters. These are personnel risks.

2. Second, they will try to win away the resources you need for short-term survival. These are immediate resource risks.

3. Third, they will try to disrupt your systems of transportation and communication. These are logistical risks.

4. Fourth, they will try to devalue the long-term investments that you have made. These are your asset risks.

5. Finally, they will try to undermine your working relationships with others. These are your organizational risks.

You have to defend all five targets. For these attacks to succeed, you must leave opponents an opening. If you fill the opening opponents target, you can block their duplication of the work you have pioneered.

It takes time for rivals to target these vulnerabilities. You must be standing still for them to catch you. Your first defense is to stay ahead of others, upgrading these assets and systems before they can be used against you.

The environment must make targeting your different types of resources easy for them. When the environment is changing quickly, you cannot always adapt as swiftly as you need to. This offers competitors a target. Do not invest in moving to new positions unless the resources on which your current position depends are secure.

You also need to keep an eye on how change is affecting your rivals. If change is making their current position untenable, they may attempt desperate measures to undermine you position. You must make sure that none of your resources offer a tempting target.

You can know when you are susceptible to climate attacks by studying the signs in your environment. You must act to cut off these attacks before they get started. If you do nothing, you are inviting these attacks.

Protect Your Relationships

The next few principles in this chapter relate to protecting relationships during times of crisis. During a climate that encourage attacks, your relationships with others are the key to meeting these attacks. You must make it difficult for competitors to undermine your key relationships. Using changing conditions to shift allegiance is the quickest way for competitors to undermine your success. The easiest way to defeat this threat is to use your relationships well.

You must win the support of others. Do not overburden these relationships. People maintain their past relationships unless given a reason to change. If you care about your relationships and keep the working with you enjoyable, people will want to stay with you if they possibly can.

Keep engaged in your relationships. You don't want lose valuable connections because they are taken for granted. Share the challenges you face with others and ask for their advice. Ask how you can work together more closely. Treat the people with whom you work like a family and treat your family better in the future than you have in the past. Your people must see that you are committed to your relationships. People judge how you will treat them by how they see you treat others.

In good times, share your success with others. Everyone should benefit from their connections with you.

In bad times, people should know that they can depend on you. They should see that you honor your commitments, even when difficulties arise.

People get nervous in times of change. You must demonstrate your confidence in the future. Supporters must respect your expertise as a leader. Sometimes, this requires confidence and detachment. You must care about your relationships, but you must not turn any relationship into a burden.

You must control what your supporters see and hear. They must believe in you without your explaining your reasoning. You can reinvent your relationships. You must be able change the enterprise's direction.

Five Forms of Attack Defense

Next, this volume looks at various forms of climate attack and how we defend against them. During times of change, everyone tries to think more competitively, that is, they start comparing their alternatives. You must prepare for five different types of competitive challenges. You must know how to adapt to them to secure your current position.

First, competitors will try a direct attack. They will want to undermine your mission at the core of your position. This requires a defense against division.

Second, competitors will an indirect attack, trying to panic those who support you. They may launch this attack through the media or through the court system. This requires a panic defense that requires that you remain calm and avoid overreaction.

Third, competitors will try an attack using openings you create. You will make mistakes. They will try to use them to undermine your position. These requires knowing how to defend openings and make things right when situations go wrong.

Fourth, competitors will try an attack to win your partners. This requires knowing how to defend alliances.

Finally, your competitors will find a tipping point to undermine your position's dynamics. This requires knowing how to defend your position's balance.

You must recognize these five forms of competitive attack. You must actively protect your positions against them. You must recognize and respond to them immediately as you do to different campaign situations.

Climate attacks are more dangerous than normal changes in the climate. Changes in the climate can undermine your position. Changes in the climate can force you to adjust your relationships. Climate attacks are different. These attacks can destroy your position completely if you do not understand the principles for response.

Do Not Overreact

The final principles in this chapter balance the dangers of climate vulnerabilities against their benefits. As we said in the beginning, these vulnerabilities are a double-edged sword. Yes, they can be used against you, but you can also use them against your opponents. To do so, however, you must understand the dangers.

Climate is the elements of emotion. During times of change, emotions run high. To balance this, these are the times when it is most important to maintain a cool head. You must not overreact to climate shifts or the attacks they make possible. Avoid letting change become an emotional issue. Your feelings about your competitors must not confuse you. Stay focused on your position.

You must respond to the situation, not to the emotion. You must defend your position, not hurt your competitors. In the long run, you beat the competition by finding new openings to advance your position. When your position is secure, you must focus on the next opportunity. Your success demands continual progress. You want to devote your mind to improving your business, not to hurting competitors. Your best defense against competitors is utilizing every opening they give you.

To be successful, you must not change your position simply to create problems for competitors. Make problems for rivals only when it helps you to do so. If there is no profit in hurting your opponents, you cannot afford to act against them. One of Sun Tzu's most basic principlesis tht you can destroy your own position in fighting your opponents.

No matter how many competitors you destroy, you will always have new competitors. If you weaken your business destroying a competitor, it is just a matter of time until the next competitor destroys you. You want to hurt competitors only when it pays to do so. You want to weaken them only when that action makes you stronger in the market as a whole. You must avoid taking actions that weaken you along with your competitors.

Any attack can be a problem, but it can also be an opportunity. You must look at every attack dispassionately, seeing whether you can turn it to your advantage. For every attack that hurts you, there will be another attack that helps you. Only your competitors can create opportunities for you.

Final Thoughts on Defending Vulnerabilities

Truly dominating positions make attacks extremely difficult. If you pick the right opportunities and build up the right positions, you can prevent competitors from even thinking about challenging you.

Competitors follow the path of least resistance. If you make what you do look difficult, they will be much less likely to copy you. It is worth the time to control appearances.

It is always easier to defend than attack. If you establish a position first, it will always be more profitable for you to defend it than it will be for competitors to attack it.

9.0.0 Understanding Vulnerability

Sun Tu's six key methods regarding the use of common environmental attacks.

"Everyone attacks with fire."
Sun Tzu's The Art of War 13:2:1

"There can be no vulnerability without risk; there can be no community without vulnerability; there can be no peace, and ultimately no life, without community."
M. Scott Peck

General Principle: We must know the five targets and five types of environmental attacks.

Situation:

This article introduces the ninth and final section of The Playbook. It covers vulnerability to environmental crises that Sun Tzu called "fire attacks." Established positions have a degree of natural security from opponents, but positions are always vulnerable to conditions in the environment. When conditions are right, opponents can use the environment as a weapon against us. In Sun Tzu's The Art of War, fire attacks were a loophole in the rule that damaging opponents is too costly to long-term success. These environmental attacks damage opponents without the risks or costs of direct conflict. In our modern world, rivals use the government, the media, or special interest groups to create these fire storms. Law suits, government investigations, and bad publicity are today's form of fire attacks or environmental attacks. Though the examples we see on the news are those directed at large organizations, most environmental attacks are directed at individuals and small organizations.

Opportunity:

Once we understand the principles of environmental vulnerability, we can use these principles not only to defend our own position, but to undermine opposing positions. All environmental attacks are attacks by proxy. The conditions and forces in the environment do the work. An opponent's role is limited only to sparking that attack, usually in a hidden way working behind the scenes. Our first concern is with defending our position against these vulnerabilities (5.6.1 Defense Priority). This knowledge also has its offensive use. The general rule here is that we must do so only to advance our own position, not simply destroy the position of another.

Key Methods:

To use the environment against an opponent, the conditions must be right.

1. The conditions for these environmental attacks depend on changes in climate to create needed fuel. This fuel in the environment is consumed to power these attacks. If we are not using environmental forces for destructive attacks, we are in a war of attrition, which means we are using our own resources and not those in the environment. This is costly and must be avoided. We cannot create these environment conditions only trigger and use them when they exist Attacks-by-proxy are not always possible. Positions must be susceptible to them. This is largely a matter of climate. Popular figures are impossible to attack. Unpopular figures are easily attacked. These attacks some times work best as attacks against individuals, other times, against faceless organizations, and still at other times, against new projects (9.1 Climate Vulnerability).

2. There are five points at which a position is vulnerable to environmental attacks. If we recognize these five targets, we can see when they are vulnerable. This recognition can be used to either defend our own position or attack our opponents (9.2 Points of Vulnerability).

3. Environmental attacks are primarily a test of leadership skills. Defense against these attacks are the single greatest test of leadership. One constant rule for defense is that we cannot panic. Overreaction usually causes more damage than the attack itself. Our decisions and reactions in these situations determine whether we maintain support for our position or create openings for our opponents *(9.3 Crisis Leadership).*

4. We must know how to defend against five types of environmental attacks. Their nature determines how we must defend against them. These details will be the topics of future articles. Different types of environmental attacks follow different courses of events, but these attacks can all be defended. Some of these attacks can even be turned against opponents that instigate them (9.4 Crisis Defense).

*5. We can use environmental attacks against other*s *only if we understand the techniques and their dangers*. We must not use these opportunities to damage the positions of others simply because we can. The goal of strategy is always to improve our own position. Simply hurting others is a waste of resources. Environmental attacks can be a dangerous two-edge sword. They can be turned against us. Most importantly, today's rivals can be tomorrow's allies (9.5 Crisis Exploitation).

6. Defending a position requires constantly monitoring our environment for vulnerabilities. Though the world is constantly changing, we are often blind to change. Both opportunities and vulnerabilities can be difficult to see. The direction of our position is much easier to see if we continually compare it to the past using the right yardsticks (9.6 t Vigilance).

Illustration:

These attacks are growing more common in today's world. Politicians, lawyers, media people, and grievance hustlers of all types have promoted this form of competitive attack. Though these groups and people are working to advance their own positions, their self-interest must be hidden. For the modern attack-by-proxy to work, the attack must be positioned for the good of society and the public. Let us look at how these attacks are used against businesses by their competitors.

1. The conditions for these environmental attacks depend on changes in climate to create the needed fuel. There is only so much public outrage. The public eventually gets bored with an issue such as global warming and moves on to some fresh outrage. Once the public moves on, the politicians, lawyers, and the rest do was well. In an anti-business climate, businesses become susceptible. In an anti-military climate, the military becomes susceptible. In a anti-politician climate, politicians are susceptible. The first rule of defense against attacks-by-proxy is keeping in touch with the social climate.

2. There are five points at which a position is vulnerable to environmental attacks. Sometimes, these attacks work against individuals, other times, against large organizations, and still at other times, against new projects whose forms of change can be made to seem threatening.

3. Environmental attacks are primarily a test of leadership skills. In the modern era, the phrase, "it wasn't the crime but the cover-up," is a common form of over-reaction.

4. *We must know how to defend against five types of environ-mental attacks*. A direct attack on core values, such as an attack on the profit incentive for large corporations, must defended differently than an attack that demonizes an individual.

5. *We can use environmental attacks against other*s *only if we understand the dangers*. Sun Microsystems instigated a series of antitrust actions against Microsoft via California politicians, but they forced Microsoft to get more involved in politics and, in the end, it was Sun that was acquired by a software company, Oracle systems.

6. *Defending a position requires constantly monitoring our environment for vulnerabilities.* In business, we must constantly be aware of how the motivations of others in the environment are changing. Politicians, lawyers, and the media constantly need fresh meat for their grinders. We must constantly shift our position to avoid becoming their targets.

9.1.0 Fire Storm Vulnerability

Sun Tzu's seven key methods describing our vulnerability to environmental crises.

"To attack with fire, you must be in the right season. To start a fire, you must have the time."

Sun Tzu's The Art of War 13:2:1

"When we were children, we used to think that when we were grown-up we would no longer be vulnerable. But to grow up is to accept vulnerability... To be alive is to be vulnerable."

Madeleine L'Engle

General Principle: Changes in climate create vulnerability to a crisis.

Situation:

Vulnerability describes an opening created by the climate, the temporary conditions in our environment that endanger our position. Vulnerability arises specifically from our position's dependence on our environment. We depend on our environment for our resources. Vulnerabilities weaken our ability to control our resources. Just as our environment contains resources, it also contains threats to those resources. These threats are the potential fuel for the problems, called fire storms, that can erupt and endanger our position. We use the term *fire storm* to connect to connect the concept of a climate crisis to Sun Tzu's original discussions of fire as a weapon.

Opportunity:

Temporary conditions are always changing. Some of these changes create the conditions in which fire storms can erupt (1.3.1 Competitive Comparison. Our opportunity is in seeing when changing climate creates the fuel for fire storms. Those who see where positions are vulnerable can know how to use conditions for defense or attack (9.1 Climate Vulnerability). If we know where these vulnerabilities lie, we lessen our risk to such threats and can leverage them against our opponents.

Key Methods:

The following key methods explain how fire storms arise and create vulnerability.

1. A fire storm requires a spark. Changes in climate create the conditions that fuel environmental vulnerability, but the presence of fuel alone doesn't start a fire. An event must trigger the crisis. While the spark can arise from natural causes, more often than not the source of that spark is created by the actions that people take or fail to take (2.3.1 Action and Reaction).

2. Some fire storms are self-inflicted wounds. These environmental crises are unintentional triggered by people who fail to understand conditions. Self-inflicted wounds arise from a failure to recognize potentially dangerous conditions and undertaking actions that trigger the danger inherent in those threats (2.5 The Big Picture).

3. Other fire storms are attacks-by-proxy. These are intentional triggered by opponents who understand conditions. Attacks-by-proxy arise from the desire to weaken a position that cannot be attacked directly (9.0 Understanding Vulnerability).

4. We maintain the safety of our position by studying the changes in our environment. If we recognize potentially dangerous conditions in the environment, we do not undertake actions that can potentially trigger the danger inherent in the situation. The best time to act to protect ourselves is before competitors can get started. If we do nothing, we make eventual problems from conditions in the environment much more likely and perhaps unavoidable (5.6.1 Defense Priority).

5. A failure to recognize dangerous conditions is often a failure of perspective. If we have a wellrounded contact network, we should get an early warning from others as these conditions develop. This is one reason why we need people in our network that see situations with fresh eyes (2.4.2 Climate Perspective).

6. A change in climate can create new opponents. We are never safe simply because we have tried to avoid creating enemies. The environment can create opponents for us. One of the ways that we are blindsided by fire storms is when we fail to see how change creates new opponents (9.1.1 Climate Rivals).

7. There are standard processes by which threats emerge. If we recognize the process by which threatening conditions normally arise, we can forecast firestorms and more frequently use them to our benefit (9.1.2 Threat Development).

Illustration:

Real life provides us many examples of people missing environment threats, both those that should be obvious and those that are much harder to foresee. Both self-inflicted wounds and attacks-by-proxy are common. Let us look at these principles from the perspective of political developments in the 2008-2012 period.

1. A fire storm requires a spark. Both Obama and then the Tea Party movement seem to have arisen almost overnight, the conditions of government over-reach and over-spending have been going on for a decade to prepare the way for it. However, it was the spark of the bail-out bills and other huge increases in spending during an economic downturn that sparked it.

2. Some fire storms are self-inflicted wounds. Politicians who fail to recognize changes in political climate often create fire storms by pushing through legislation that enrages the public. After unpopular bailout and stimulus bills, the climate and health care bills are self-inflicted wounds, triggering outrage.

3. Other fire storms are attacks-by-proxy. New laws often make novel attacks that are impossible to foresee. For example, the Endangered Species Act enabled radical environmentalists to hobble both new development and traditional economic activity such as farming and logging by pressing the government into protecting little known species like the spotted owl or snail darter.

4. We maintain the safety of our position by studying the changes in our environment. The gradual increase in spending, debt, government regulation justified by the environment or security have been going on the US for quite a while.

5. A failure to recognize dangerous conditions is often a failure of perspective. In politics, the winners seem to think they get into office based upon their own virtues rather than the mistakes of their opponents. First the Republican and then the Democrat Party misinterpreted the signs. The same frustration with government that cost the Republicans Congress and then the Presidency is now being ignored in the same way by the Democrats.

6. A change in climate can create new opponents. In politics, only a relatively few are more influenced by a political party than they are by the general political climate. Politicians, like sports teams, have "fair weather" supporters who quickly turn on them as conditions deteriorate.

7. There are standard processes by which threats emerge. The balancing of forces of politics can stay in the middle for a long time, but threats emerge as conditions work toward the extremes of complementary opposites.

9.1.1 Climate Rivals

Sun Tzu's six key methods for preparing against how changing conditions create opponents.

"Your rivals will multiply as your army collapses and they will begin against you."
Sun Tzu's The Art of War 2:1:20

"One man with 100 loyal friends is a lot stronger than one man with 1000 dead enemies, but only the former knows it, and only the latter cares."
Gregory Wallace Campbell

General Principle: Changes in climate can turn others into opponents.

Situation:

We normally think about changes in climate creating new opportunities, but such changes can also create new opposition as well. Strangely enough, both improving and worsening conditions can change former allies into opponents. Our vulnerability is to conditions in our environment, but rivals and opponents play a critical role in transforming those conditions into a fire storm against us. The danger is that we do not understand who our potential enemies are, trusting current allies for the wrong reasons. That danger is magnified as conditions get more challenging because we can too easily give them the time to use those conditions against us.

Opportunity:

Changes in climate creates new opponents but they also create the potential for new alliances. Current allies can become rivals and current rivals can become friends. Both opposition and alliances arise ultimately from our goals and values (1.6 Mission Values). According to Sun Tzu's competitive elements, Climate does not control mission, but its does change mission priorities (5.1 Mission Priorities). A downturn in the economy, for example, increases the importance of our financial concerns. This change of goals shifts who our friends and enemies may be.

Key Methods:

The following key methods explain how climate can create enemies.

1. Environmental changes can create enemies when new dangers arise. Changing conditions can force former allies to compete with one another. Tough times shift allies toward the broader, more basic concerns of physical preservation (1.4.1 Climate Shift).

2. Environmental changes can create enemies when dangers are removed. Diverging goals can change former allies into opponents. Good times shift allies toward the narrower, more personal issues of personal fulfillment and idealism (1.6.1 Shared Mission).

3. In tough times, we must create a common enemy, amplifying the danger to unite people. We must clarify the shared mission, specifically avoiding the dissipating situation. The challenge in dealing with tough times arising from fire storms is maintaining support (9.3.1 Mutual Danger).

4. During good times, we must expect ties to weaken and new rivalries to develop. We must protect our vulnerabilities from potential new opponents. This is one of the ways that good times create tough times (3.2.5 Dynamic Reversal).

5. Alliances are often more threatened by good times than bad. Good times create new rivalries. Old friends know our vulnerabilities better than most opponents. In exploiting our vulnerabilities, new rivals can create fire storms against us. These fire storms can lead to tough times (9.2.5 Organizational Risk)

6. Used correctly, we can use fire storms to bring people together. When conditions get more challenging, we can focus everyone on mutual defense. Since defense takes a priority over offense, we are drawn together by our mutual aversion to loss (9.3.1 Mutual Danger).

Illustration:

Let us look at a couple of simple examples of how enemies can be created in good times and bad.

1. Environmental changes can create enemies when new dangers arise. When a company announces that it is going to be downsizing, former business friends and partners are transformed into rivals and competitors, when they realized that they are competing directly with each other to maintain their position.

2. Environmental changes can create enemies when dangers are removed. In business, when a company is booming, partners who once struggled together against the common enemy of the marketplace can turn on each other. There is only room for one leader in an organization and as organizations grow, jealousies and contests for dominant positions naturally erupt.

3. In tough times, we must create a common enemy, amplifying the danger to unite people. When a sports team is losing, everyone starts looking for who to blame. The owner, coach, and star player who were once the best of friends are suddenly in a contest that requires them defending their positions against each other.

4. During good times, we must expect ties to weaken and new rivalries to develop. The history of Apple Computer offers a great example of this power struggle. First there was Jobs and Wozniak. When Jobs became dominant, he brought in Sculley from Pepsi. Sculley then pushed Jobs out. Job eventually made his way back. All of this, however, during one of the great business success stories.

5. Alliances are often more threatened by good times than bad. As the hi-tech market expands into new areas, Google, Microsoft, and Apple find themselves competing more seriously in more areas, even though they have all worked together in the past.

6. Used correctly, we can use fire storms to bring people together. The threat of government regulation, such as the regulation of the Internet by the FCC, often brings serious rivals such as Google, Microsoft, and Apple together.

9.1.2 Threat Development

Sun Tzu's seven key methods on how changing conditions create environmental threats.

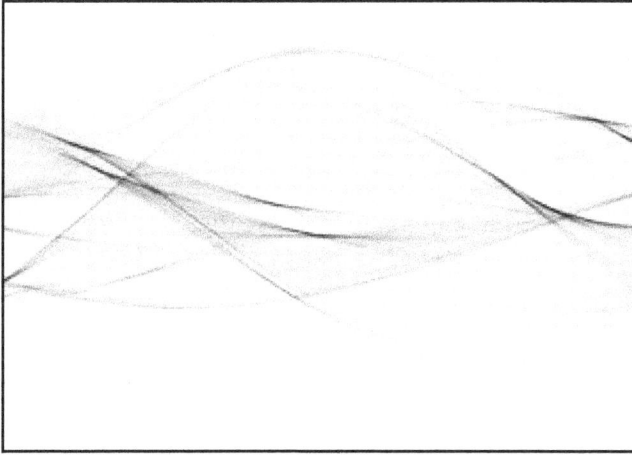

"Use discipline to await the chaos of battle.
Keep relaxed to await a crisis."
Sun Tzu's The Art of War 2:1:20

"When did the future switch from being a promise to
being a threat?"
Chuck Palahniuk

General Principle: Changes in climate can turn others into opponents.

Situation:

The vulnerabilities that undermine an established position seem to come from out of nowhere. We seem suddenly blind-sided by an unexpected crises. But is that really true? Our vulnerability to conditions in the environment come largely from our false expectations of stability. If something has remained the same for any period of time, we come to expect it to continue to remain the same indefinitely. Where there is change, we falsely expect it to continue in the same direction. This is simply not the way the real world works. The problem is that our expectations have been warped by our training in linear thinking.

Opportunity:

Our opportunity comes from recognizing that progress doesn't flow in a straight lines but changes directions, dictated by the forms of the environment not the wishes of men. The certainty of chaos is predictable. As Sun Tzu says, "Chaos gives birth to control." His strategy teaches the limits of knowledge and control. From those limits, we can predict that: 1) all attempts at controlling the environment will eventually fail (3.2.1 Environmental Dominance); 2) progress in one direction will be eventually balanced by natural opposing forces (3.2.3 Complementary Opposites); 3) any emptiness will be filled and every fullness will be emptied (3.2.4 Emptiness and Fullness); and 4) the longer a trend continues, the more dramatic the reversal can be (3.2.4 Emptiness and Fullness). Notice, these predictions are about what will happen not when it will happen.

Key Methods:

This knowledge allows us to foresee the environment changes that result in our vulnerabilities. This knowledge dictates a process cycle creating these vulnerabilities that we can recognize. The patterns follows clear stages:

1. Threat development starts with a period of stasis ending in a change. Conditions in the environment change in some way. A new law is passed. A new perspective or meme begins to spread. A new technology is introduced (1.1.1 Position Dynamics)

2. The change creating a threat evolves so slowly that we become complacent. When people first notice it, change may worry them, but after awhile it seems innocuous. Life continues as before.

Any predictions of threat from the change seem incorrect. People cry "wolf" and "the sky is falling" so often that real dangers in change are lost among false ones (7.5.2 The Spread of Innovation).

3. *The threat goes through a long accumulation stage where the potential for crisis builds to a breaking point.* Over time, change creates more and more resources for fueling the eventual fire storm. This fuel can take a variety of forms, from the building of negative opinions to the increase of bad tangible assets. Since a little of this fuel doesn't seem to be a problem, people, reasoning linearly, don't worry about its accumulation (1.2 Subobjective Positions).

4. *As the fuel for a crisis accumulates, early warnings are easy to ignore.* There are a few, sporadic events that indicate that a fire storm can result from the accumulation of fuel, but these events are minor and result from very uncommon events. They are easily written off because people see them as "non-typical." This is the point at which those trained in Sun Tzu's Playbook should recognize that fuel is accumulating in the environment and start erecting defenses (2.4.2 Climate Perspective).

5. *The fuel in the environment builds to a flash point where crisis is unavoidable.* The accumulation of fuel reaches the point where fire storms are easily sparked. The situation goes through a *phase transition* where any common, typical event can have a very different result than the past. Opponents begin to see that they can use these conditions against each other (1.3.1 Competitive Comparison.

6. *A defense against the crisis must be mounted.* After the flash point, the dangers become clear. People are forced, often against their will, to react to the situation. They erect defense against the dangers of the fuel that has accumulated in the environment (3.2.1 Environmental Dominance.

7. *The danger wanes and the environmental threat diminishes.* The situation rebalances itself in one of two ways. If defenses work, protection becomes universal. If defenses do not work, but the number of fire storms eventually depletes the accumulated resources necessary to bring a situation to the flash point (3.2.3 Complementary Opposites).

Illustration:

Let us look at this pattern to examine the latest financial crisis. I personally used this pattern recognition to get all of my assets out of the financial markets by August of 2008, protecting them from the fire storm.

1. Threat development starts with a period of stasis ending in a change. The changes from in the Community Redevelopment Act (CRA) promoting "affordable mortgages (1993-1998), the Sarbanes Oxley bill (2002) making IPOs more difficult for investment banks, and the bundling of "affordable mortgages" as investment instruments first by Fanny and Freddy (2005) and then by investment banks seeking new products to replace IPOs.

2. The change creating a threat evolves so slowly that we become complacent. During the growing economies of the 90s and early 21st century, the relatively small numbers of loan defaults made the new sub-prime mortgage investments seem safe. AIG begins to insure these instruments against loss.

3. The threat goes through a long accumulation stage where the potential for crisis builds to a breaking point. The number of bad assets mount in the system. Government policy gradually increases the required percentage of "affordable mortgage" loans made by banks. Soon these loans account for hundreds of billions and then trillions of dollars of assets. The accumulation was 4.7 trillion by 2007.

4. As the fuel for a crisis accumulates, early warnings are easy to ignore. In 2007, Lehman Brothers was liquidated, Bear Stearns and Merrill Lynch were sold at fire-sale prices, and Goldman Sachs and Morgan Stanley became commercial banks. General public is unaware of the problem.

5. The fuel in the environment builds to a flash point where crisis is unavoidable. During September 2008, the crisis hits its most critical stage triggering a run on the markets. Lending in all forms slows dramatically. Nearly one-third of the U.S. lending mechanism was frozen and continued to be frozen into June 2009.

6. *A defense against the crisis must be mounted.* Banks increase credit requirements for loans. People pull their money out of markets, increasingly distrusting government assurances.

7. *The danger wanes and the environmental threat diminishes.* Not yet. While standards have been tightened, the fuel of the bad loans, including many questionable commercial loans, is still in the environment.

9.2.0 Points of Vulnerability

Sun Tzu's five key methods on our points of vulnerability during an environmental crisis.

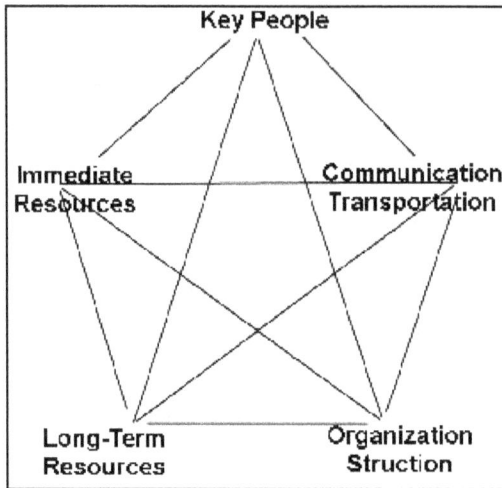

Key People

Immediate Resources

Communication Transportation

Long-Term Resources

Organization Struction

"There are five ways of attacking with fire."
Sun Tzu's The Art of War 12:1:1

"Upon the creatures we have made, we are, ourselves, at last, dependent."
Johann Wolfgang von Goethe

General Principle: There are five key points of vulnerability in every position.

Situation:

Once we have successfully claimed a valuable position, we must protect it against environmental threats. Environmental fuel can be sparked by chance, accident, or intentionally into fire storms that can undermine our position. To defend our position, we must defend all the points at which we are vulnerable to these threats. Enmity and vulnerability arise from changes of conditions in the environment (9.1 Climate Vulnerability). Vulnerability doesn't threaten a position as much as it threatens the resources on which a position depends. The danger is that many of us don't identify the resources on which we are dependent. If we don't consciously know our dependencies, we will almost certainly fail to see the dangers that threaten them before they arise.

Opportunity:

If we understand the resources on which our position depends, we can see threats to those resources before they mature, and actively work to secure those resources against those threats. If we understand the resources on which our allies and opponents depend, we can use that knowledge to secure our alliance and endanger our enemies. Though destruction is always easier than creation, it is much less costly to defend existing resources than it is to recreate them (1.8 Progress Cycle).

Key Methods:

Our position depends on five of types of resources. These five key sets of resources are listed in their order of importance. The five points of vulnerability are also are five key points of defense. They are:

1. The primary targets for threats are the key individuals whose decisions maintain our position. This group includes ourselves, but its also includes others such as our spouse, key employees, and bosses whose play a key role. If these people are threatened by a environmental crisis, our position is also threatened (9.2.1 Personnel Risk).

2. The second most critical targets to protect are the immediate resources we need to be productive. These include the assets, the raw materials, and equipment that we need immediate access to on a day-to-day basis. If we lose these assets, we cannot be productive until we replenish them. these are the same resources we need in excess to explore new opportunities (9.2.2 Immediate Resource Risk).

3. The third most important targets to protect are our communication and transportation network. Communication and transportation provide the flow of resources, including decisions, to where they are needed (9.2.3 Transportation/Communication Risk).

4. The fourth most important targets to protect are our fixed, longer term assets. These include our storage of excess resources and any resources that can be converted or transported to be used as immediate resources (9.2.4 Asset Risk).

5. The fifth most important target to protect is our organizational structure. The organization structure consists of the arrangement of activity, responsibility, and authority. Systems of organization divide responsibilities to increase the effectiveness of organization. (9.2.5 Organizational Risk).

Illustration:

Let us look at these five categories of targets from the perspective of business, personal life, and military conflict.

1. The primary targets for threats are the key individuals whose decisions maintain our position. In business, these are our key employees, suppliers, and customers. In our personal life, these are our spouse, family, and friends. In the military, these are our troops and supporters in the field.

2. The second most critical targets to protect are the immediate resources we need to be productive. In business, these are our cash on hand and cash flow. In our personal life, these are our cash, food, water, etc. on hand., In the military, these are food, ammunition, and other supplies in the field.

3. The third most important targets to protect are our communication and transportation network. In business, these are our transportation, communication, and information systems. In our personal life, these are our car, phones, computers, highways, etc. In the military, these are communication, transportation, and logistic systems.

4. *The fourth most important targets to protect are our fixed, longer term assets.* In business, these are the fixed assets used for production and storage. In our personal life, these are our house, savings, and so on. In the military, these are our stockpiles of supplies and national production systems.

5. *The fifth most important target to protect is our organizational structure.* In business, these are our business organization extending to suppliers and marketplaces. In our personal life, these are our neighborhood, community, and other local resources. In the military, these are our military bases and alliances.

9.2.1 Personnel Risk

Sun Tzu's five key methods on the vulnerability of key individuals.

"The only correct move is to preserve your troops."
Sun Tzu's The Art of War 10:3:19

*"Once a Marine, always a Marine. The challenge
and the camaraderie with players and coaches,
no one experiences anything like that but in team
sports, especially football. It's almost like a chemical
dependency. Whereas losses used to destroy them, now
they have the wisdom to be able to move on easier."*
Bill Walsh

General Principle: Our position requires us to protect the individuals on which it depends.

Situation:

If we don't understand exactly how Sun Tzu's concept of our strategic position depends on others, we cannot understand how to defend our position during a crisis. We depend on both the generic roles of groups and the unique roles of key individuals. Individuals are more susceptible to attacks than groups. As individuals, people can be isolated and attacked personally on many different levels: physically, mentally, emotionally, and spiritually. Groups can be attacked from outside only on the physical level: on their financial or physical base of support. If the individuals on which we depend are vulnerable, then we are vulnerable. We are especially vulnerable if we depend on the support of only a few, key people.

Opportunity:

In the end, half of our strength comes from sharing the goals of others (1.7.1 Team Unity). Without the support of others, even our victories can seem hollow, meaningless. When we share the journey with others, even setbacks can increase our strength (6.8.2 Strength in Adversity). It is safer to depend on groups for the physical resources and on key individuals for our intellectual, emotional, and spiritual support. While our support from groups can depend on the support of key individuals within that group, most individuals in groups can come and go because group interactions are often based on standard methods not individual character (1.5.2. Group Methods). The difference between an anonymous group and an organization to which we belong is the presence of a key individual who acts as the leader (1.5.1 Command Leadership).

Key Methods:

To defend our position, we must defend both our relationship with groups and our relationships with key people. We must also know when our relationship with the group depends on specific key people with their organizations. To defend the people on who we depend, we must:

1. Know the key relationships on which we depend. We cannot defend everywhere. We must focus on defensive resources on where they matter most (5.5 Focused Power).

2. Keep our key relationships secret. Attacks are more effective focused on individuals. We want to deny others a focus for their attacks (2.7 Information Secrecy).

3. Understand the motivations of these key individuals. We must understand their priority to understand where they are vulnerable (1.6.3 Shifting Priorities).

4. Recognize the individual weaknesses of key individuals. These weaknesses can provide the inspiration and the basis for personal attacks (4.7.1 Command Weaknesses).

5. Keep close enough to key individuals to know when they are the most susceptible to the attacks. Attacks are only damaging to people when they are launched when they are in a personally vulnerable position (1.4.1 Climate Shift).

Illustration:

What does it mean to depend upon a group instead of individual? As a business, it means to depend upon an anonymous group of customers instead of one, specific large customer. As an employee, it means depending upon a group of coworkers who may change as individuals. A key individual's role is different. For example, a business relationships with an entire group of buyers can depend on the good opinion of one key buyer to who the others look for guidance. As an employee, though we depend upon a changing group of coworkers to do our job, we may also depend upon the good opinion of our boss as the key individual to keep our job.

Examples of defending or failing to defend key individuals:

1. Know the key relationships on which we depend. Investors in Apple computer or BerkshireHathaway have to think about what happens to the value of their stock if Steve Jobs or Warren Buffet comes under attack from, for example, a disease.

2. *Keep our key relationships secret.* President Obama's personal relationships with those like Professor Gates or his former past, Jeremiah Wright change the nature of the discussion when they are public.

3. *Understand the motivations of these key individuals*. When a high-profile attorney like Mark Geragos is hired by a defendant like Scott Peterson, the defendant needs to understand that the attorney's primary interest is in self-promotion and winning the case is secondary to that goal.

4. *Recognize the individual weaknesses of key individuals*. Political leaders such as Bill Clinton, Newt Gingrich and John Edwards hurt their entire cohort because of their personal flaws regarding marital fidelity.

5. *Keep close enough to key individuals to know when they are the most susceptible to the attacks*. In Bill Clinton's case, the warning signs were there for years, but those close to him ignored those signs until the situation became a crisis.

9.2.2 Immediate Resource Risk

Sun Tzu's five key methods on the resources required for immediate use.

"Without supplies and food, your army will die."
Sun Tzu's The Art of War 7:2:19

"Time is more valuable than money. You can get more money, but you cannot get more time."
Jim Rohn

General Principle: We must protect the resources we need to maintain our current activities.

Situation:

All positions require resources to maintain them. If we do not have the resources our position requires, we cannot defend it. In terms of our vulnerability, our most common resource limitation is time. All positions require time to maintain them. Some positions require other immediate resources as well to keep them productive, such as energy, money, or raw materials. If these required resources run out, the position quickly begins to fail. How quickly they fail depends how quickly a position consumes resources for production. When these resources are consumed or destroyed by an environmental crisis, our position immediately becomes vulnerable. While these resources are used within an organization, the realm of planning , they come in from outside the organizations, the realm of strategy. While we have some control over our supplier relationships, our control is limited.

Opportunity:

An environment crisis can not endanger our immediate resources as long as we recognize the danger and respond appropriately. Positions normally consume immediate resources at a predictable rate. If we are concerned about our vulnerabilities, we pay attention to what we need rather than take immediate resources for granted. We line up alternative sources for resources. This is true even for time. Our personal time is limited, but there are almost seven billion people in the world, many of whom can exchange their time for other resources that they need. Though none of us get more than 24 hours in a day, we can increase the time we have by getting help from other people. We defend our immediate resources by assuring their continued flow during a crisis.

Key Methods:

To defend the immediate resources on which our positions depend, we must:

1. To protect the vulnerabilities of our immediate resources, we must identify those resources. Each position depends on different types of resources. We must know the types of resources on which our position depends (3.1.1 Resource Limitations).

2. To protect our immediate resource, we must know their rate of consumption. All resources are limited. We can only defend a position when we know what its maintenance requires (8.7.1 Evaluating Erosion).

3. To protect our immediate resource, we must keep our needs and their sources a secret. This is simply a matter of controlling information on a need to know basis (2.7 Information Secrecy).

4. To protect our immediate resource, we must always have alternative sources for them. We must never base our position on a single source of support. We must also know when a transition from one source to another will create its own vulnerability. A key part of developing positions is resource discovery ([nodecontent/761-resource-discovery link]).

5. To protect our immediate resource, we must know what excess resources can be exchanged for them. Good strategy requires us to accumulate excess resources for expansion but they are also used to eliminate vulnerabilities (3.3 Opportunity Resources).

6. To protect our immediate resource, we must keep a close watch on needed resources when climate changes. These changes are the precursor of all environmental attacks. The first sign of the dangers of an environmental attack can be the dwindling of resources (1.4.1 Climate Shift).

Illustration:

The most obvious example of this rule is a business position.

1. To protect the vulnerabilities of our immediate resources, we must identify those resources. A factory requires a flow of raw materials. A restaurant requires a flow of food. Businesses require a flow of money to pay their recurring expenses. Salespeople require a flow of new prospects, products, and promotions. Relationships require a flow of contact, communication, and moments. Our health requires a flow of exercise, nutrition, and rest. Sometime, the key resources are not obvious. For example, it is obvious that an army needs ammunition, but food and water is even more important because it is needed more often. As Napoleon observed, an army travels on its stomach.

2. *To protect our immediate resource, we must know their rate of consumption.* We must know the rate at which a given position consumes these liquid resources. What value of raw materials are needed to keep the factory running at current capacity? What volume of food does the restaurant need? What volume of case does the businesses require? How many new prospects, products, and promotions does a salesperson need? How much time does a relationship take?

3. *To protect our immediate resource, we must keep our needs and their sources a secret.* A business competitor can target a key supplier.

4. *To protect our immediate resource, we must always have alternative sources for them*. When a business, army, or individual depends upon a single supplier, its vulnerability increases. Of course, the one resource always affected by an environmental attack is time. Defending ourselves from a law suit, an IRS audit, bad publicity and so one always consumed time. Since time is limited, an attack in our position in one area can rob time and focus from another: a challenge at work can hurt our relationships at home and, reversing the view, problems in our relationship can rob time at work.

5. *To protect our immediate resource, we must know what excess resources can be exchanged for them*. While businesses usually assume that money can be exchanged, when supplies run short, prices goes up. We must consider other forms of exchange, such as exchanging time, getting needed resources today in exchange for a long-term contract, for example.

6. *To protect our immediate resource, we must keep a close watch on needed resources when climate changes*. When a key part of the environment changes, such as the recent change in healthcare laws, businesses and other organizations much pay closer attention to that area because it can be the source of new environmental attacks.

9.2.3 Logistics Risk

Sun Tzu's four key methods on how firestorms choke normal channels of movement and communication.

"If you make your army travel without good supply lines, your army will die."

Sun Tzu's The Art of War 7:2:18

"Logistics and transportation are among the many critical functions that rely on our converged communications network."

Doug Gardner

General Principle: We must protect our channels of communication and transportation from a change crisis.

Situation:

All positions depend on the flow of resources and information that we call logistics. These paths are potential choke points. A break anywhere in the path destroys its utility. Our vulnerability in transportation and communication only becomes visible during environmental "fire storms". This vulnerability is especially visible during the rare firestorms that panic the public. During such a panic, communication lines and transportation systems are jammed and unusable. Smaller scale firestorms, such as a denial of service attacks on a internet server, are much more common but much less visible forms of the same concept.

Opportunity:

The systems through which resources and information flows are networks which means that alternative paths are available(2.4 Contact Networks). Between any two points, there are any number of potential lines. Certain transportation and communication paths may work better but there are also other paths which can be used. Firestorms serve a purpose in highlighting the weaknesses in these systems. Communication and transportation systems are in our areas of "control" (1.9.2 Span of Control). We only recognize their unpredictability when their capacities are tested in a flare-up of competition (1.9.1 Production Comparisons).

Key Methods:

To defend our position, we must protect our need for a continuous flow of information and resources, but we also must understand that during a climatic firestorm, special methods apply to using those channels.

1. To defend communication/transportation vulnerabilities, we must not get panicked into using these channels unnecessarily. This is the first rule because it is our first reaction as part of the "flight or fight reflex". We conserve needed immediate resources by avoiding an expensive but unnecessary reaction (9.2.2 Immediate Resource Risk).

2. *To defend communication/transportation vulnerabilities, we must use alternative channels during a crisis.* It is best to address this challenge before a crisis arises. We must find the openings rather than following the crowd. (3.1.4 Openings).

3. *To defend communication/transportation vulnerabilities, we must move or communicate based on our needs.* We must not move or communicate simply because a crisis arises. Firestorms do not last so it is a mistake to change our position based on them. Our choice of action and nonaction must be dictated by the needs of our position not merely by what is happening at the moment (5.1.1 Event Pressure).

4. *To defend communication/transportation vulnerabilities, we can choose less rather than more.* The choice of actions or non-action is always central to good strategy. In facing the specific challenges presented by environmental firestorms, both being panicked into action or frightened into silence are both very common mistakes (4.2 Choosing Non-Action).

Illustration:

Let us look at the common mistakes that are made in communication and transportation during firestorms. The mainstream media provides us with a stream of "panics" that illustrate these principles. Indeed, we might say that the media itself has too often become choked with panics, preventing it from providing real new.

For our illustration, let us use a panic from last summer as our example, so we have a little strategic perspective on it, the "crisis" of high gas prices.

1. *To defend communication/transportation vulnerabilities, we must not get panicked into using these channels unnecessarily.* Instead of conserving gas by traveling less, people wait in lines at cheaper stations, buying gas before the price goes up whether they need it or not at the time.

2. To defend communication/transportation vulnerabilities, we must use alternative channels during a crisis. During a gas shortage or price panic, people waste gas in rush hour traffic instead of going into work earlier and avoiding the crowds.

3. To defend communication/transportation vulnerabilities, we must move or communicate based on our needs. The biggest mistakes of the gas shortage were made by the companies that decided to base their advertising campaigns on it. Those commercials about high gas prices were still running during the next firestorm, the financial meltdown, making those companies look silly and out of touch.

4. To defend communication/transportation vulnerabilities, we can choose less rather than more. When fuel prices go up, we should travel less and communicate more. It is always cheaper to move information than material.

9.2.4 Asset Risk

Sun Tzu's four key methods regarding the threats to our fixed assets.

> *"If you don't save the harvest, your army will die."*
> Sun Tzu's The Art of War 7:2:20

> *"You are your greatest asset. Put your time, effort and money into training, grooming, and encouraging your greatest asset."*
>
> Tom Hopkins

General Principle: We must protect our long-term, fixed assets during a crisis.

Situation:

Time may be our most valuable resource, but it doesn't last. If we cannot transform our time into longerterm resources, we will always be poor. The beauty of youth is a great example of a resource that cannot last. However, our reputation never gets old. A firestorm highlights the vulnerability of our long-term assets since they are usually not portable or quickly converted into other assets. What we build up over a lifetime, we can lose in a short-term change of climate.

Opportunity:

Long-term assets are the most easily defended aspects of our position (1.1.2 Defending Positions). Their stability give them a permanence that we can use to our advantage. Owning a long-term assets is a commitment. We cannot easily walk away from it. When it is endangered by a climatic threat, our mission to protect it should be crystal clear.

Key Methods:

The first rule of protecting long-term assets is that we must accept the job as our personal responsibility. Though it may be the formal responsibility of a set of professionals to protect us, it is always a mistake to abdicate our responsibility to them. No one cares as much about our assets as we do.

1. We work in advance to remove any potential fuel for threats to longer-term assets. For our assets to be hurt by a climate change, the threat must be based on an issue with ownership or legality. We must identify and remove these threats to assets long before a problem arises (9.1.2 Threat Development).

2. When a threat arises, we must expend immediate resources to protect long-term assets. During danger periods all excess resources must be converted into a form we can use for defense. (9.2.2 Immediate Resource Risk).

3. When a threat arises, we must mobilize others who have similar assets at risk. A group is always more powerful than an individual alone. A threat to similar long-term assets creates a powerful shared mission. We can use our shared mission to work together to protect our assets during a crisis (1.6.1 Shared Mission).

4. If the resource as a whole cannot be saved from a threat, we must rescue any parts that we can. Sometimes the nature of the calamity is such that it cannot be stopped. In that case, we must save what we can even if we cannot save everything (5.0 Minimizing Mistakes).

Illustration:

As an example, let us think about a home being threatened by a wildfire (9.1 Climate Vulnerability).

If our house is threatened by a wide-spread wildfire, we shouldn't expect firefighters to save it. During a wildfire, firefighters have bigger priorities that saving our house. We do not.

1. We work in advance to remove any potential fuel for threats to longer-term assets. If we live in a fire zone, we should keep the brush away from our house, put on a roof that is fire proof, and perhaps even make sure we have additional water supplies on hand.

2. When a threat arises, we must expend immediate resources to protect long-term assets. If we can borrow a water tanker, we should make the investment.

3. When a threat arises, we must mobilize others who have similar assets at risk. Sometimes, it is easier to protect our house by protecting the neighborhood. If the house next door is burning, we have a real problem. One person cannot create a fire break on their own, but a group of neighbors can.

4. If the resource as a whole cannot be saved from a threat, we must rescue any parts that we can. If the fire is going to claim the house, we can still save the dog.

9.2.5 Organizational Risk

Sun Tzu's five key methods on the targeting the roles and responsibilities within an organization.

> *"An organized force is braver than lone individuals. This is the art of organization."*
>
> Sun Tzu's The Art of War 11:4:18-19

> *"Responsibility is the price of greatness."*
>
> Winston Churchill

General Principle: Crises threaten organizations by undermining confidence in management ability.

Situation:

By definition, dealing with climatic threats fall outside the normal channels of organizational responsibility. During a firestorm, the chaotic, confusing external competitive environment intrudes directly into the normally orderly world of planning and organization. The normal result in organizations is fear. While organizations are less vulnerable than individuals to an environment attack, such attacks create a crisis of confidence. A dramatic, threatening change in climate arises, people's faith in the organization is often shattered. The threat of the firestorm is then amplified by the organizational chaos.

Opportunity:

When a firestorm descends on an organization, there is an opportunity to demonstrate our strategic vision in a way everyone can appreciate. If we want to move up in the organization, it is an opportunity to demonstrate our strategic skills. Trained in organization, design, and planning for controlled environments, most managers tend to panic during breakdowns of control, when an adaptive response is required. A unplanned threat provides a perfect showcase for those who can work confidently outside of the span of control (1.9.2 Span of Control). People at every level of the organization above us and below us will tend to follow our lead if we have been trained in what an environment challenge requires.

Key Methods:

To protect confidence in the organization during an climatic firestorm, we must step up to exercise or assume command guided by the following key methods.

1. We protect the organization's vulnerabilities by remaining calm and exhibiting decisiveness during a crisis. This is the single most important important role of a leader during a crisis. Even the choice of doing nothing if that is what is required must be made decisively (9.5.2 Avoiding Emotion).

2. We protect the organization's vulnerabilities by mobilizing resources to protect assets at risk. We identify the five areas of vulnerability that need safeguarding and know the steps necessary for defending them (9.2 Points of Vulnerability).

3. We protect the organization's vulnerabilities by winning people's support during a crisis. During danger periods all excess resources must be converted into a form we can use for defense (9.3 Crisis Leadership).

4. We protect the organization's vulnerabilities by responding correctly to the five methods of using firestorms. This is simply a matter of knowing the specific defensive key methods for each situation (9.4 Crisis Defense).

5. When the threat of crisis passes, we must switch from defense to offense. We must quickly rebuild or recapture any parts of the organization's position that were lost or damaged (5.6 Defensive Advances).

Illustration:

We have many recent political examples of poor jobs of handling a firestorms, usually by politicians--from which we have gotten the phrase, it's not the crime its the cover-up, but let us look at a positive example. One of the best jobs of defending the credibility of an organization during a firestorm was the work of Johnson & Johnson during the Tylenol scare of October, 1982. This firestorm arose from the news that someone had poisoned Tylenol capsules in the first major case of product tampering. When the crisis struck, no one knew how, where, or how many the pills had been poisoned.

If our house is threatened by a wide-spread wildfire, we shouldn't expect firefighters to save it. During a wildfire, firefighters have bigger priorities that saving our house. We do not.

1. We protect the organization's vulnerabilities by remaining calm and exhibiting decisiveness during a crisis. Management responded immediately and decisively, without a hint of defensiveness, showing none of the "flight or fight" behavior that less capable leaders usually demonstrate.

2. *We protect the organization's vulnerabilities by mobilizing resources to protect assets at risk*. Management immediately recognized that their most important asset was their reputation, especially the reputation of the leading product in its category. They immediately spent $100 million dollars recalling and destroying their entire stock of product everywhere.

3. *We protect the organization's vulnerabilities by winning people's support during a crisis.* J & J management treated their customers like members of their own family, exactly what is required during a crisis,

4. *We protect the organization's vulnerabilities by responding correctly to the five methods of using firestorms.* They did what was required and, despite the size of the crisis, they left their opponents no opening for attack.

5. *When the threat of crisis passes, we must switch from defense to offense.* The product was relaunched with a new triple-sealed package, a huge discounting program, and 2,250 sales people sent out to reassure medical people. In the end, the Tylenol product won market share through its good PR instead of losing it.

9.3.0 Crisis Leadership

Sun Tzu's nine key methods for maintaining the support of our supporters during attacks.

> *"Winning a battle is always a matter of people."*
> Sun Tzu's The Art of War 4:5:1

> *"The crisis of today is the joke of tomorrow."*
> H. G. Wells

General Principle: Win people's support during periods of vulnerability by understanding competitive psychology.

Situation:

Periods of crisis have a huge impact on our relationships. Even when our supporters are not the target of these threats, a crisis threatens our relationships with others. Even when those relationships have nothing to do with our authority within an organizational structure, fire storms pose a real risk to the trust and confidence that others place in us. Climatic change and a sudden threat from the environment creates fear and uncertainty. This surge of emotion often results in psychological desire to find someone to blame. One danger is that our rivals can use these periods of vulnerability to steal away our supporters, but these crises threaten relationships on a more basic level. Relationships have inertia. People stay in their current relationships unless they are given a reason to leave. If we don't manage our relationships correctly, a crisis can be the catalyst that destroys our relationships.

Opportunity:

Crises are always an opportunity to bring people closer together. They provide dramatic, memorable moment that, when handled correctly, can be a solid foundation of shared experience that can last lifetime. To navigate the immediate crisis, we must leverage relationships with others correctly, but our relationships are more important than the crisis. The crisis won't last, so we must see our relationship from a perspective that goes beyond the immediate danger. If we care about the people who are key to our position, people will want to stay with us. These situations have the potential to generate conflicts (9.1.1 Climate Rivals), but they can also generate a shared mission of survival.

Key Methods:

We cannot take people's support for granted. We must win their support every day.

1. We should let others depend on us in a crisis. People need a leader and we should always be ready to assume the role. When people depend on a leader, they lose their fear of the situation. If people depend on us, they will then defend us instead of abandoning us when challenges get difficult (1.5.1 Command Leadership).

2. In a crisis, we must communicate clearly, frequently, and send the same message to everyone. We can stop less people from worry and second-guessing us by making our messages clear. The more frequently that we make contact, the closer our relationships become. We must control what our supporters see and hear so we know what they are thinking (9.3.2 Message Control).

3. In a crisis, w e must emphasize the common threat to solidify the group. The challenge is to increase our sense of shared mission when others might try to destroy it. If rivals want to use our problems to steal our supporters, we should make our supporters feel that competitors are threatening them personally (9.3.1 Mutual Danger).

4. In a crisis, w e want to create a sense of belonging and family. We must make people see our groups as unique and special. Our people must see that we are committed to them and we must demand commitment back. People often judge how we will treat them by how they see us treat others (1.6.1 Shared Mission).

5. In a crisis, w e must give others a mission and a role to play. When people are busy, the lose their fear. When they have a role, they feel valuable. When we give people challenging work to do, they will pay attention and be part of the solution instead of the problem. If they can advance there position working with us, they will stay with us (1.6.2 Types of Motivations).

6. In a crisis, w e must emphasize how we depend on each individual in the group. No one should see themselves as baggage. Without being told, everyone should be asked to contribute for their mutual benefit. Without being asked, everyone must see what is needed. Without being monitored, our supporters will prove that they can be trusted (1.7.2 Goal Focus).

7. In a crisis, people should be partnered with others to minimize their weaknesses. More experienced people should be made responsible for less experienced people. By combining our efforts, we are all stronger (1.7.1 Team Unity).

8. In a crisis, w e must channel our emotions and avoid partiality. Leadership requires our confidence and detachment. We must care about our people, but we cannot let ourselves get wrapped up in their emotional issues (8.5 Leveraging Emotions)..

9. *After the crisis, we must share our success with others.* People want to be rewarded for being part of the team. The more transparent we can make our organizations rewards, the happier people are. If people are in the dark about rewards, they will imagine that they are being left out (8.0 Winning Rewards).

Illustration:

What should a business person do when his or her industry is threatened with an evironmental attack, for example, from a special interest group pressing for more destructive government regulation?

1. *We should let others depend on us in a crisis.* If you want to be seen as a leader, you should immediately contact everyone else in the industry to offer a clear vision for dealing with the situation.

2. *In a crisis, we must communicate clearly, frequently, and send the same message to everyone.* The leader should be clear about the problems of government and specific about how they can be mitigated and minimized by group response.

3. *In a crisis, w must emphasize the common threat to solidify the group.* The leader should create a way for his or her different competitors and those related to get together and work together through their common problem.

4. *In a crisis, w e want to create a sense of belonging and family.* When the business leader gets others within the industry together, he or she should give their association a name that promotes the positive benefits their industry offers to their customers, an identify to set them apart from the rest of the market that is affected by the crisis.

5. *In a crisis, w e must give others a mission and a role to play.* The business people starting the organization should identify the specific actions each member can take roles to help mitigate the problems of the crisis identifying specific people that can communicate a shared point of view with 1) their employees and customers in their marketplace to make it clear that they have a stake in the situation, 2) the industry media, local media, and general media, and 3) the government or other controlling organizations.

6. In a crisis, w e must emphasize how we depend on each individual in the group. The association should identify the best role for each member, giving the most important roles to the most important and visible members of their industry.

7. In a crisis, people should be partnered with others to minimize their weaknesses. The association cannot let its larger, more visible members to be targeted and isolated from the group. Large members have more resources, but smaller members have the advantage of numbers and distribution. Both types of members are valuable.

8. In a crisis, w e must channel our emotions and avoid partiality. The association must not panic so that one group sells out another. When it comes to government regulation, larger members usually sell out smaller because the larger organizations can bear the costs of regulation more than smaller. However, smaller members can sell out larger organizations, letting them draw direct attacks.

9. After the crisis, we must share our success with others. When the crisis passes, the industry will go back to competition, but it is best that they set up a permanent self-policing and lobbying organization to prevent future crises that draw government attention.

9.3.1 Mutual Danger

Sun Tzu's six key methods describing how we use mutual danger to create mutual strength.

"To command and get the most out of proud people, you must study adversity."

Sun Tzu's The Art of War 11:4:12

"The Chinese use two brush strokes to write the word 'crisis.' One brush stroke stands for danger; the other for opportunity. In a crisis, be aware of the danger - but recognize the opportunity."

Richard M. Nixon

General Principle: Leaders focus attention on the common enemy to create team unity and focus.

Situation:

While we use Sun Tzu's methods to do our best to avoid dangerous situations, we cannot avoid crisis. Crisis creates mutual danger. Mutual danger threatens the survival of both organizations and, in the worst cases, individual lives. The two biggest dangers during a crisis is panic and division. Panic results in bad decisions, but division creates new forms of conflict that worsen the danger. If we want to avoid division, we must understand how to use a crisis.

Opportunity:

When the crisis eventually comes, we must use it as as an opportunity to generate the sense of unity and focus that creates strength. A loving God created a world full of danger, pain, and trouble so that we would need one another. Sun Tzu used the analogy of men in a boat in a during a storm to capture the character of our mutual danger. In the face of mutual danger, people find a way to work together easily and naturally because of their shared mission (1.6.1 Shared Mission). Used correctly, the danger of crisis maximizes our strength. Sun Tzu teaches the strength of any group (1.7 Competitive Power) comes from the unity of its members (1.7.1 Team Unity) and their focus on a single, clear mission (1.7.2 Goal Focus). Shared danger is the opportunity to create a powerful shared mission of survival (1.6.1 Shared Mission).

Key Methods:

Under the methods for dealing with a crisis, the third rule is, "In a crisis, we must emphasize the common threat to solidify the group." (9.3 Crisis Leadership). There are six key methods for accomplishing this correctly.

1. The methods for highlighting mutual crisis must be used only in times of real danger. Like the boy who cried wolf, if we inflate every minor issue into a crisis, we will find that these powerful methods work less and less well over time, and, when we need them, they will be unavailable (6.0 Situation Response).

2. During a crisis we must focus attention on the objective and concrete aspects of shared danger. We want to generate energy, not fear. People are afraid of the unknown, but the more tangible the enemy is, the more it concentrates the mind. (1.2.0 Subobjective Positions).

3. During a crisis we must make it clear that flight is not an option. We want people to face the crisis, not turn their backs on it. If people cannot run away, the only remaining instinctive mindset is to fight (2.3.3 Likely Reactions).

4. During a crisis we must accentuate that everyone is united against the danger. When people see themselves as part of a group, they also feel greater safety. There should be a sense that the greater danger is in leaving the group rather than staying together (6.8.2 Strength in Adversity).

5. During a crisis we must use the danger as an incentive to action. Whether we want people to hold our current position or move that position, seeking safety during a time of danger must be the highest priority (1.6.3 Shifting Priorities).

6. During a crisis we must emphasize the risks, costs, and the certainty of success. The danger isn't really a danger if there are nothing at risk. The costs are reasonable because of the risks. The certainty of success must arise from the unity and focus of the group (1.5.2 Group Methods).

Illustration:

In our recent times,.no one has used these ideas better than Churchill during World War II. We study his famous speeches during the period, and we see each of these principles being used clearly and concisely.

1. The methods for highlighting mutual crisis must be used only in times of real danger. Politicians and the media today have so consistently violated this rule and we are seeing the inevitable result. When everything is a crisis, from global warming to corporate profits, nothing is a crisis. Churchill, of course, had tried to get people to pay attention the real danger of Germany before WWII, with no affect.

2. During a crisis we must focus attention on the objective and concrete aspects of shared danger. Churchill did such a good job of making the enemy concrete that Hitler and the Nazis are still synonymous with evil.

3. During a crisis we must make it clear that flight is not an option. Churchill: "Never give in. Never give in. Never, never, never, never--in nothing, great or small, large or petty--never give in, except to convictions of honor and good sense. Never yield to force. Never yield to the apparently overwhelming might of the enemy."

4. During a crisis we must accentuate that everyone is united against the danger. Churchill ended his first speech as prime minister in 1940: "But I take up my task with buoyancy and hope. I feel sure that our cause will not be suffered to fail among men. At this time I feel entitled to claim the aid of all, and I say, 'Come then, let us go forward together with our united strength.'"

5. During a crisis we must use the danger as an incentive to action. Churchill in his "their finest hour" speech after the fall of France and the evacuation at Dunkirk: "During the first four years of the last war the Allies experienced nothing but disaster and disappointment. That was our constant fear: one blow after another, terrible losses, frightful dangers. Everything miscarried. And yet at the end of those four years the morale of the Allies was higher than that of the Germans, who had moved from one aggressive triumph to another, and who stood everywhere triumphant invaders of the lands into which they had broken. During that war we repeatedly asked ourselves the question: 'How are we going to win?' And no one was able ever to answer it with much precision, until at the end, quite suddenly, quite unexpectedly, our terrible foe collapsed before us, and we were so glutted with victory that in our folly we threw it away.

6. During a crisis we must emphasize the risks, costs, and the certainty of success. Churchill: "Do not let us speak of darker days:

let us speak rather of sterner days. These are not dark days; these are great days--the greatest days our country has ever lived; and we must all thank God that we have been allowed, each of us according to our stations, to play a part in making these days memorable in the history of our race."

9.3.2 Message Control

Sun Tzu's five key methods on communication methods to use during a crisis.

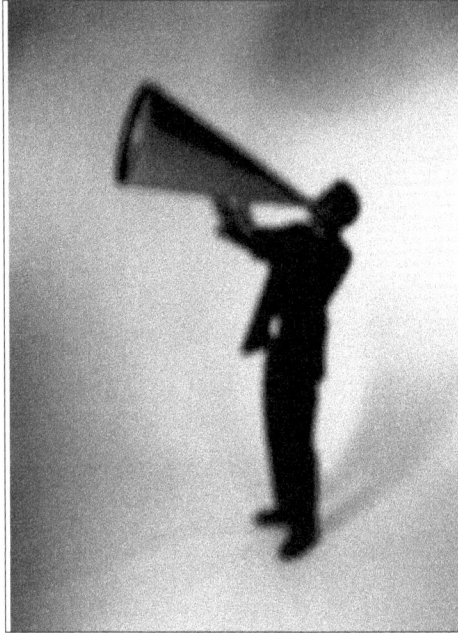

"You must position your people to control what they see and hear."

Sun Tzu's The Art of War 7:4:14

"Good communication does not mean that you have to speak in perfectly formed sentences and paragraphs. It isn't about slickness. Simple and clear go a long way."

John Kotter

General Principle: Leaders focus attention on the common enemy to create team unity and focus.

Situation:

The real danger during a crisis is always in our response. Nothing in that response is more critical than the messages that we send. During a crisis, people are overloaded with too much conflicting information. The chaotic conditions of the external environment disrupts the orderly flow of productive communication. Because of the high noise to message ratio, individuals can easily receive very different messages regarding the situation. When people have very different perspectives on a situation, they are likely to choose different responses. As people go in different directions, unity breaks down, diluting the effectiveness of every action.

Opportunity:

A single, clear voice can rise above the cacophony of the situation. A simply message can create a rallying point. The right message sent in the right way creates the unity (1.7.1 Team Unity) and focus (1.7.2 Goal Focus)required to generate the excess strength necessary to get through a crisis (1.7 Competitive Power). When we handle a crisis well, it always improves our position afterward. This is especially true about the subjective impressions that others have about our position. Those subjective impressions can be translated into objective rewards.

Key Methods:

Under the key methods for dealing with a crisis (9.3 Crisis Leadership), the second rule is, "In a crisis, we must communicate clearly, frequently, and send the same message to everyone." The following five key methods describe the process.

1. Crisis communication must keep messages about response short and simple. During a crisis, time is short and there is already too much information. Bandwidth is limited. We must use our limited resources wisely (3.1.1 Resource Limitations).

2. Crisis communication must repeat a consistent message over and over. Unless we repeat the message, most people will miss it because of competing distractions. On each repetition, we reach more people (7.4.1 Timing Methods).

3. *Crisis communication must amplify and dramatize the message*. Amplification is not only a matter of volume, but of using a variety of methods, pictures as well as sounds. (1.5.2. Group Methods).

4. *Crisis communication must use a perspective that reaches everyone equally*. When creating our message, we have to find a common denominator. We have to ask what everyone's different experiences have in common (2.0 Developing Perspective).

5. *Crisis communication must make it easy for people to signal their position*. Communication is not just a one-way street. We must have ways of knowing if people received the message and can respond. The easier we make it to respond, the easier it will be to keep everyone on the same page (5.4 Minimizing Action).

Illustration:

For concrete examples, let us look to our political class for examples of what happens when these principles for message management are violated. Though the defining health care situation as a crisis violates the first rule of using danger, since the Obama administration defined it that way, we can use this standard for evaluating their message. Since passage of the health care law, the sinking popularity of Obama, Democrats, and government leading to the loss of the House in 2010 demonstrates the danger of ignoring these principles.

1. *Crisis communication must keep messages about response short and simple*. A 2,000+ page health care bill is a long and complicated response that violates this rule.

2. *Crisis communication must repeat a consistent message over and over*. Not only was there one such bill, but about five competing versions so no one even knew what the response was. Even the repeated mantra "health care crisis" morphed into "health insurance crisis" and finally into "we will know what is in it when it passes."

3. Crisis communication must amplify and dramatize the message. The message was amplified using the bully pulpit of the White House, but its opposition was what was dramatized on the streets and town hall meetings.

4. Crisis communication must use a perspective that reaches everyone equally. The chosen message only made sense to those who thought that a government solution was an obvious solution and that spending more public funds is never a problem. This message missed middle America who does consider spending a problem and that government is as often the problem as the solution.

5. Crisis communication must make it easy for people to signal their position. Rather than understand where people were to develop a common perspective, the administration was much more interested in cutting off discussion.

9.4.0 Crisis Defense

Sun Tzu's five key methods on how vulnerabilities are exploited and defended during a crisis.

"Every army must know how to adjust to the five possible attacks by fire."

Sun Tzu's The Art of War 12:2:17

"Any fool can have bad luck; the art consists in knowing how to exploit it."

Frank Wedekind

General Principle: We must recognize the five ways our adversaries can use a crisis against us.

Situation:

Our type of vulnerability to an environment crisis depends on the methods used against us. When opponents work to spark a crisis, we can only defend by responding with the right counter measures. A crisis can weaken us temporarily, but inappropriate responses can destroy us completely. Opponents can try to spark a crisis in five different ways. Each of these different methods works to create a different type of mistake. These methods seek to either 1) create division; 2) cause panic; 3) use an opening; 4) damage alliances, or 5) tip a balance.

Opportunity:

If we are trained in crisis response, we know that there are only five different ways our vulnerabilities can be exploited during these situations. We can prepare against these five different forms of competitive challenges in the same way that we defined the five targets for these attacks: targeting our vulnerabilities (9.2 Points of Vulnerability). If we respond appropriately to these five different forms of sparking and using a crisis, these situations offer little danger (6.0 Situation Response). Situation response, as always, requires two components 1) identifying the situation, and 2) reflexively reacting appropriately. As with all of strategy, we must know how to adapt to them to continuously defend any valuable position.

Key Methods:

There are five key methods for recognizing and responding to opponents' efforts during an environmental crisis.

1. When opponents seek to create division during a crisis, we defend our periphery. When environmental conditions threaten our uniting mission, they will actively work to pick off our weakest and most distant supporters by targeting those furthest from us, geographically or philosophically (9.4.1 Division Defense).

2. When opponents seek to exploit panic during a crisis, we avoid overreactions. Opponents rely upon our overreactions to environmental challenges. If we remain calm in the face of an environment challenge, they will not challenge us. If we panic, they will jump into the fray, using our negative momentum against us in any way that they can (9.4.2 Panic Defense).

3. When opponents want to use an opening created by the crisis, we must fill it first. It takes time for crisis damage to create an opening, so opponents must wait to use it. They patiently watch as our problems with the external environment reach their peak and then they use the opening that the damage creates (9.4.3 Defending Openings).

4. When opponents hope to win our allies during a crisis, we must protect our key relationships. During a fire storm, allies can attempt to distance themselves from us for fear of "guilt by association." We must actively work to protect our allies from any spillover during the crisis. Otherwise, our opponents will use the crisis as evidence of our indifference and try to win our allies and other key relationships away from us. (9.4.4 Defending Alliances).

5. When our competition is evenly balanced, adversaries will use a crisis to tip the balance in their favor. When a temporary trend arises in a competitive arena, either side of an evenly matched contest can take advantage of it. The side that recognizes the opportunity first can use it as a tipping point shifting the basis of competition 9.4.5 Defensive Balance).

Illustration:

Below we offer different examples from business and politics for each of these five methods.

1. When opponents seek to create division during a crisis, we defend our periphery. For example, when Apple saw the Microsoft's Vista release was getting attacked in the media, they directly attacked the Vista operating system and tried directly to divide off those customers who were the least devoted to Windows.

2. When opponents seek to exploit panic during a crisis, we avoid overreactions. Consider the problems that companies can have with a product recall. If a company panics, such as the ***Peanut Corporation of America*** did in <u>trying to initially cover up their salmonella problem</u> in 2008 and 2009, they are finished. When a company doesn't panic and acts decisively, as Johnson & Johnson did during the cyanide scare of the eighties, they maintain their position easily (<u>9.2.5 Organizational Risk</u>).

*3. **When opponents want to use an opening created by the crisis, we must fill it first.*** We saw a good example of this technique during the last election as the Democrats leveraged unhappiness with the war in Iraq when it was at its height. They started working when this opening was created, before the surge. Though the surge can only be considered a success, the opening created by unpopularity with the war gave the Democrats control of congress and eventually the presidency.

*4. **When opponents hope to win our allies during a crisis, we must protect our key relationships.*** In sports, for example, coaches will often support an unpopular or under-performing player for the sake of the team as a whole. When this happens, the coach's opponents can undermine his or her position by keeping the focus and pressure on these weaker players.

*5. **When our competition is evenly balanced, adversaries will use a crisis to tip the balance in their favor.*** There was a great example of this technique in the Obama/McCain campaign. In the week before the vote, the financial crisis arose. McCain, after his initial panic (see number 2 above) suspending his campaign could have used the crisis to win the election by opposing the bailout, which was unpopular in both parties. Instead, Obama laid blame for the crisis at the Republicans door and McCain by failing to blame the Democratic Congress and, most importantly, by siding with Obama in supporting the bailout, gave up any chance of tipping the balance in his favor and lost the election.

9.4.1 Division Defense

Sun Tzu's five key methods for preventing organizational division during a crisis.

"You start a fire inside the enemy's camp. Then attack the enemy's periphery."

Sun Tzu's The Art of War 12:2:3-4

"Leaders must be close enough to relate to others, but far enough ahead to motivate them."

John Maxwell

General Principle: To avoid division, leaders must rally to their people.

Situation:

People seek the safety of organizations during times of crisis. Opponents can actively work to split people off from an organization. They do this by putting the group, its leaders, or its mission at the core of the crisis. Done correctly, this transforms the organization from a haven to a threat for its members. This use of a crisis is possible because one of the key vulnerabilities of groups is the distance separating the people. This distance can be either physical or psychological. Opponents can pick off the weakest and most distant by targeting those furthest away, either geographically or philosophically.

Opportunity:

A crisis gives leaders an opportunity to prove the value of their organization. During a crisis, leader prevents division by understanding strategic distance (4.4 Strategic Distance). This is especially important in large organizations where division is a natural consequence of size (3.4.1 Unity Breakdown). The mutual danger created by the crisis is a powerful tool for leaders (9.3.1 Mutual Danger) The sense of shared danger among the members of the organization is an opportunity to bring them all together into a shared point of view. The strength of an organization is its unity (1.7.1 Team Unity).

Key Methods:

Sun Tzu offers these principles to avoid panic during a crisis.

1. During a crisis, we protect our mission defending our supporters. This means moving closer to those who are being engaged by our adversaries. Nothing says more about the shared power of the mission than our willingness to defend others. (1.6.1 Shared Mission).

2. During a crisis, we focus our message on the value of our shared effort. The crisis is temporary while our goals will go on. Our progress toward our goals is still part of our position. We must use all of the techniques of message control to communicate the value of our shared defense (9.3.2 Message Control).

3. During a crisis, we emphasis the safety in working together especially for the most distant. Since our opponents will start trying to divide us working at the periphery, we reach out to those at the periphery. We make sure to include them in our message of shared mission, danger, and safety in numbers (9.3.1 Mutual Danger)

4. During a crisis, we use organized activities to give people an outlet. People are united by actions. If we give people activities to perform, it provides a focus for the emotional energy generated by the crisis. They must feel responsible to the group to feel that the group is responsive to them (6.5.1 Dissipating Response).

5. During a crisis, we address the organizational damage quickly. The worst danger is ignoring people's concerns with the organization. The more quickly we can get the crisis under control and behind us, the more meaningless opposition attacks become (6.1.1 Conditioned Reflexes).

Illustration:

As an example, let us examine Microsoft's response to the problems created by its 2005 release of the Vista operating system. This situation created the fuel for a crisis of confidence, which Apple sparked by their "I am a Mac and I am a PC" advertisements. While the Microsoft's problems with Vista fall into the category of a crisis from self-inflicted wounds, their response to the attack by Apple was a demonstration of solid strategy. This quality of response has been less common for Microsoft in recent years.

1. During a crisis, we protect our mission defending our supporters. Microsoft's response was to defend its users, who Apple, in selling their own cool were clearly using the crisis climate. Some videos here.

2. During a crisis, we focus our message on the value of our shared effort. Microsoft's "Windows versus walls" emphasized Apple's love for proprietary control.

3. During a crisis, we emphasis the safety in working together especially for the most distant. Microsoft had both the advantages and disadvantages of size. While Mac emphasized their cool, Microsoft emphasized their affordability for the masses, which reached the broadest group of people.

4. During a crisis, we use organized activities to give people an outlet. Instead of pushing Vista, Microsoft chose to emphasize the Windows brand. They took a number of steps to make it easier for people and organizations to stay with XP. This was a good decision compared with their normal methods for encouraging the use of the new operating system by limiting backward compatibility.

5. During a crisis, we address the organizational damage quickly. Windows 7 came out in record time and a record low price. Windows 7 built on the Windows brand and fixed the many visible shortcomings of Vista making it much easier for people to move on with Microsoft rather than leave.

9.4.2 Panic Defense

Sun Tzu's four key methods to prevent the mistakes from panic during a crisis.

> *"You launch a fire attack, but the enemy remains calm. Wait and do not attack."*
>> Sun Tzu's The Art of War 12:2:3-4

> *"Doubts and mistrust are the mere panic of timid imagination, which the steadfast heart will conquer, and the large mind transcend.*
>> Helen Keller

General Principle: To avoid panic, leaders must stay calm and know how to calm others.

Situation:

The greatest danger from a crisis is emotional over-reaction. People can attack us more easily for our bad reactions than they can on the basis of a crisis alone. We are not responsible for the external conditions that provide fuel for the crisis or our opponents' actions that sparked those conditions into a crisis, but we are always responsible for our responses. A crisis, by definition, falls outside of normal, expected conditions. Since most of us are not trained to respond to unexpected conditions we panic, that is, overreact out of the fear of the unknown. When we panic, we create a great opening for our opponents to attack us, even when the crisis itself does not.

Opportunity:

Training in Sun Tzu's methods are the ultimate protection against panic. His entire science is dedicated to dealing with situations where we must make decisions quickly under uncertain conditions with limited information. A crisis gives us the opportunity to demonstrate how "chaos gives birth to control," as Sun Tzu teaches. When we demonstrate our strategic leadership in a chaotic situation and improve how others perceive us, which is the key to improving our position over all (1.2 Subobjective Positions).

Key Methods:

The following principles describe how we defend ourselves and our organizations against panic.

1. To prevent panic during a crisis, we must reach out to our contact network. People tend to panic more when they feel isolated. This contact discourages panic in both directions. It decreases our own fear and the fears of those we contact (2.4 Contact Networks).

2. To prevent panic during a crisis, we must see uncertainty as normal. While we expect good information within our span of control, we must accept that most of the world lies out our control. We cannot let what is unknown spark fear because almost all of the universe is unknown. In a crisis, events normally run ahead of information, and we should make it clear to others that this is expected. Limited information doesn't stop us from responding and adapting our response as we learn more (2.1.1 Information Limits).

3. To prevent panic during a crisis, we must take visible actions. In Sun Tzu's system, leveraging knowledge means knowing when secrecy is required and when communication is required. Since people are more afraid of what is hidden. Secrecy and cover-ups always compound problems and increase panic. Visible action gives us an outlet for emotions and decreases panic. It is better to get information out as quickly as possible to demonstrate our confidence and ability to act decisively (2.1 Information Value).

4. To prevent panic during a crisis, we must act quickly and decisively but in scale with the problem. We use speed and visibility to create a sense of decisiveness, but we must keep reactions in proportion to the immediate dangers. While we must act, we must not over-react. This is consistent with Sun Tzu's entire philosophy of minimizing mistakes. The tendency in emotionally charged situations, especially those where people want to see action, is to do too much and create mistakes. A crisis is one of the many situations where less done quickly is usually more (5.4 Minimizing Action).

5. To prevent panic during a crisis, we must return to the enduring values of mission. The crisis is temporary. The shared mission is what matters. If we act consistently with our higher and the enduring aspects of our mission, those actions will increase confidence rather than diminish it (1.6 Mission Values).

Illustration:

We can use this as an opportunity to contrast the responses of Peanut Corporation of America trying to cover up their 2008-2009 salmonella problem and Johnson & Johnson response during the Tylenol cyanide scare of the eighties (illustration used in 9.2.5 Organizational Risk). The first was a clear example of panic while the other was a clear example of calm.

1. To prevent panic during a crisis, we must reach out to our contact network. The peanut people seem to be hiding from the story while the J & J people got in front of it on day one.

2. To prevent panic during a crisis, we must see uncertainty as normal. While neither side knew the dimensions of the problem, J&J didn't let that stop them from taking action. The peanut people, on the other hand, used the lack of information as an excuse not to take action.

3. To prevent panic during a crisis, we must take visible actions. This is where the peanut people made their biggest mistakes. The cover-up of internal problems became the entire basis of their response. While J&J didn't know where the investigation would lead, they opened their doors to investigators, confident that they would deal with any problems.

4. To prevent panic during a crisis, we must act quickly but avoid over-reactions. In a situation of public health where lives are in immediate danger, speed is critical, as J&J realized in immediately taking all their products off the shelves. It is hard to over-react in saving lives except when our reactions endanger more lives.

5. To prevent panic during a crisis, we must return to the enduring values of mission. In the end, J&J turned the crisis into a PR victory that is still getting them good reviews not only in articles like this, but in business schools across the nation. The peanut people? Not so much.

9.4.3 Defending Openings

Sun Tzu's four key methods on how to defend openings created by a crisis.

"*The fire reaches its height. Follow its path if you can. If you can't follow it, stay where you are.*"

Sun Tzu's The Art of War 12:2:7-9

"*Illusion is an anodyne, bred by the gap between wish and reality.*"

Herman Wouk

General Principle:

Adversaries will use openings created by our missteps during a crisis if we let them.

Situation:

We created openings during a crisis by mistakes and mismanagement. In other words, we make the wrong choices. These errors are unavoidable. Sun Tzu's strategy defines an opportunity as an opening. A crisis fueled by environmental conditions our mistakes that can create openings through which our opponent can attack us. An additional problem is that we cannot predict exactly where these openings will occur. If we knew what mistakes we were making, we wouldn't make them. Not knowing where a mistake might do its damage makes it difficult for us to defend ourselves. Though we cannot predict where we will create an opening, we can predict when our opponents' will move against us. When the situation has done its maximum damage. Our opponents are hoping that we are too consumed in dealing with internal damage control to recognize our external vulnerability.

Opportunity:

In dealing with openings within our positions, we always have the advantage of proximity. Our opponents must wait to attack to see where the mistakes will occur. Since we are closer to our situation than they are, we are always better positioned recognize a mistakes and plug an opening before they can act (4.4 Strategic Distance). Our opportunity is in our readiness to surprise opponents with an instant response, recognizing our own errors (6.1.1 Conditioned Reflexes). Done correctly, we can turn the situation around so that the crisis damages them in their mode of open attack more than it hurts us in our defensive mode.

Key Methods:

To deal with the openings created by our own mistakes

1. As we shift resources to deal with a crisis, we must know what weak points we are creating. An opening is a gap in the resources that we need to maintain our position. The first way in which an opening arises during a crisis is through our own actions, as we move resources to deal with the crisis. Every strength creates a corresponding weakness. To protect against a crisis, we reinforce certain areas and thereby weaken others. Such gaps may be unavoidable, but the mistake is not being aware of it. We must do this consciously to prepare to opposition attacks (3.5 Strength and Weakness).

2. As the crisis progresses, we must know where resources are lost or damaged. This is the second way in which openings as a gap in resources are generated by a crisis. This mistake is taking the lot resources and capabilities for granted, assuming we still have them. We must be aware of the five points of vulnerability to know where we are being damaged by the crisis so that we can prepared to defend ourselves (9.2 Points of Vulnerability).

3. As the crisis progresses, we can use deception proactively to cover up our weak points. If opponents believe that we are prepared for them at the point of attack, they are less likely to attack. The mistake is letting our real internal problems appear externally as weaknesses. It is easier and less costly to prevent attack than to defend against it. We must find ways to communicate a state of readiness, especially when it doesn't exist, to discourage attacks (2.1.3 Strategic Deception).

4. As the crisis reaches its peak, we must ready a rapid defense team to move. The mistake here is not having reserves. Despite our best efforts, we may not see the opening until our opponents use it and we must have resources ready to respond (3.3 Opportunity Resources).

Illustration:

We saw a good example of this technique during the 2008 US election cycle as the Democrats leveraged public unhappiness with the war in Iraq when it was at its height. They started working when this opening was created, before the surge. Though the surge can only be considered a success, the opening created by unpopularity with the war gave the Democrats control of congress and eventually the presidency. Let us look at the weaknesses of Republican's strategy.

1. As we shift resources to deal with a crisis, we must know what weak points we are creating. While the surge tipped the balance in Iraq, the Republicans did not seem to even recognize the change in climate that made it into a handicap.

2. As the crisis progresses, we must know where resources are lost or damaged. The war in Iraq did the most damage to the Republican channels of communication (9.2.3 Transportation/Communication Risk) concerning the value of winning in Iraq. The administration was traumatized by their earlier non-response to "Mission Accomplished" attacks and never recovered.

3. As the crisis progresses, we can use deception proactively to cover up our weak points. Instead of a non-claim of non-victory, the Republican candidates should have laid the groundwork for a conservative anti-war plank. They could have discussed the surge in terms of larger endgame of disengagement. Ron Paul demonstrated how a conservative could be pro-defense but against the idea of a long-lasting war on fiscal grounds. Like Nixon's "secret plan to win" in Vietnam, this policy could have ended up maintaining the status quo while claiming to be a new approach. This is exactly what Obama's has done in Iraq and Afghanistan, continuing existing policies while claiming to do something new.

4. As the crisis reaches its peak, we must ready a rapid defense team to move. The Republicans and the Bush administration were extremely poor in responding in anything like a timely manner to Democratic attacks, whether those attack were warranted or not.

9.4.4 Defending Alliances

Sun Tzu's five key methods for dealing with weakness by association.

"Spreading fires on the outside of camp can kill.
You can't always get fire inside the enemy's camp.
Take your time in spreading it."
Sun Tzu's The Art of War 12:2:10-12

"What I don't appreciate - and what I'm confident the
voters will reject - is the attempt by some of the media
and others to engage in guilt by association."
Ralph Reed

General Principle:

Unless dealt with quickly, weakness-by-association undermines positions over time.

Situation:

A crisis can be used against our position even when the controversy isn't about us directly. We can be damaged by a fire storm of controversy through our alliances with others. This is an interesting threats because it can affect us even if we are completely innocent. Weakness or, as it is more commonly known, guilt by association can easily become a slow, bleeding wound. Initially, we can make the mistake of thinking of them as minor nuisances but they don't go away weakening our position over time. Any defense against "weakness by association" attacks must deal with incomplete information. As that information slowly comes out, the damage to our position mounts over time. We also cannot control what our associates do, which can hurt us despite our best attempts to defend them.

Opportunity:

The good news is that weakness by association attacks do not instantly get us in trouble. As always, everything depends upon our response. There is a certain unfairness about guilt by association that people initially resist. This means that these threats require time to develop into threats against us. Because of this perception of unfairness, these attacks can be turned around against our attackers. To do this successfully, we have to react quickly and discover the right defense, which depends on information about the crisis that we may not have. The attacks also give us a real opportunity to clarify our values. Our goals and values are the core of our position. We should welcome any opportunity to talk about those values. These firestorms are always about the past, past actions of past associates. What is important going forward is our values. The past cannot be changed, but we can always learn from it, especially about the importance of values.

Key Methods:

The best strategy here starts with avoiding the common mistakes in weakness-by-association attacks. The most common mistakes are:

1. When an ally faces a crisis, we must initially refuse to speculate and point out the danger in speculation. We must be clear about the dangers of false accusations and guilt by association. We must not instantly rush to defend or attack an ally when we don't know the facts. Defense of the guilty is a self-inflicted wound, transforming our ignorance into injury. Attack makes us look disloyal and foolish if the facts end up clearing our ally. It may also support the values of our opponents when they are not our values (2.1.1 Information Limits).

2. When an ally is in a crisis, we must instantly admit what we did and did not know. We cannot ignore the crisis of an ally for too long. This makes us look like we are hiding something. Since the damage seems minor, we can hope they will simply disappear, but over time our opponents can point to our reticence as evidence of guilt, and, as every bit of new information that comes out provides new fuel for the fire. If we should have recognized a problem, we can admit it and identify the signs we missed specifically, and sincerely apologize, but we can safely add the minor caveat that we always want to think best of our friends. (2.1.2 Leveraging Uncertainty).

3. When an ally has a crisis, we must keep all statements short but cover everything that must be covered. We must say what needs to be said and be willing to answer questions but avoid going on and on. Saying more than we need to say is as bad as saying nothing. We need to address the attack and quickly, but saying too much leads almost inevitably into one of the other errors (5.4 Minimizing Action).

4. When an ally is in a crisis, we must avoid dishonestly distancing ourselves from the relationship. This invites more exposures of those associations. This shift the issue from our allies misdeeds to our dishonesty (1.5.1 Command Leadership).

5. When an ally is in a crisis, we must make a clear distinction between our values and those of our opponents. This uses the crisis as an opportunity. A crisis is dangerous because it is used and often triggered by opponents, who by definition, have very different values. If our allies are accused of violating our values, we can defend those values strongly without attacking an ally who may or may not be guilty. If these attacks are really against our values, we must defend those values, strongly and clearly, against the attackers. While more people can agree with vague platitudes, values only have impact when connected to the specifics of a situation (1.6.3 Shifting Priorities).

Illustration:

During the 2008 election, candidate Obama dealt with questions about past associations. Unfortunately, he did so less than adequately and it could have cost him the election had McCain not given him the election by mishandling the financial crisis in the weeks before the vote. Questions about Obama's associations didn't cost him the election, but they set up the slow bleed that has weakened his position over time.

1. When an ally faces a crisis, we must initially refuse to speculate and point out the danger in speculation. If candidate Obama didn't know the facts, which is what he claimed at the time, he should have said nothing, reserving judgment. Instead, he defended Wright only having to repudiate him later.

2. When an ally is in a crisis, we must instantly admit what we did and did not know. Obama's unwillingness to discuss his relationships kept this story alive. This controversy built to such a degree that candidate Obama ended up making an entire speech about race to address it.

3. When an ally has a crisis, we must keep all statements short but cover everything that must be covered. While his speech about race was praised highly in the mainstream media, what does anyone remember about that speech today other than the "throwing his grandmother under the bus" moment. Obama said that he could not repudiate Wright, but then he did repudiate him only a few weeks later.

4. When an ally is in a crisis, we must avoid dishonestly distancing ourselves from the relationship. New connections between President Obama and various individuals and groups continues to be interesting because those associations are only discussed specifically by Obama's opponents.

5. When an ally is in a crisis, we must make a clear distinction between our values and those of our opponents. The biggest mistake then and now was not getting specific about what was learned from past associations and how his future associations are going to be different. During the campaign, he should have specifically addressed how Wright's ideas are wrong for the future. He should have contradicted Wright's specific statements and called them clearly racist and used that to emphasize his mission of moving on from partisan and racial divisions of the past.

9.4.5 Defensive Balance

Sun Tzu's four key methods for using short-term conditions to tip the competitive balance in a crisis.

*"Set the fire when the wind is at your back.
Don't attack into the wind."*
                    Sun Tzu's The Art of War 12:2:17-18

*"Trends, like horses, are easier to ride in the direction
they are going."*
                                    John Naisbitt

General Principle:

During a crisis, we can flank opponents or be outflanked ourselves by utilizing the onrushing trends of change.

Situation:

Fuel for a crisis builds up slowly in our environment until a spark triggers it into a firestorm. The flames of the crisis, however, are fanned by the short-term trends in the environment. A crisis amplifies the dangers of positioning ourselves against even the slightest trends. Normally, we position ourselves considering the stronger and longer-lasting conditions of the ground: gravity (4.3.1 Tilted Forms) and long-term flow (4.3.2 Fluid Forms) when meeting opposition. During a crisis, however, we must also consider the less powerful and short-term trends of climate: the shifts of emotion and fad.

Opportunity:

These short-term trends can work just as easily for us as against us. As with using the advantages of the ground, using the shifts of climate are largely just a matter of knowing which way the wind is blowing. If we flank our opponents correctly, we can not only prevent opposition attacks from starting, but turn any attacks that they try back on them. These situations also create the opportunity for surprise, where we can feign a vulnerable position to invite and attack and then reveal our true position.

Key Methods:

The strategy here is easy to understand and, when the opportunity is there, simple to execute:

1. During a crisis, we must know which way the trend is going. Another way of saying this is know which way the wind is blowing. This usually requires more than sticking up a finger up in the air. Local conditions can be misleading, so we need to get a broader perspective from the sources that we have cultivated (2.4 Contact Networks).

2. During a crisis, we must make a judgment about how long the trend will last. By definition, these are all short-term trends, but they must persist long enough to make a move worthwhile. Generally, more visible trends involve more people. The more area a trend covers, the longer it will last. (3.1.6 Time Limitations).

3. During a crisis, we must know where opponents stand. It is our position relative to our adversaries that is important. We want the direction of the trend to support our position against our opponents Until they have taken a position, we cannot take a favorable stand (1.3.1 Competitive Comparison).

4. During a crisis, we must angle into a position that puts the trend behind us and against our opponents. This usually requires a minimum of movement, just getting the angles right (5.4 Minimizing Action).

Illustration:

There was a great example of this technique in the final days of Obama/McCain 2008 presidential context, again, as is usual with politics, a great illustration of the bad strategy rather than good. In the week before the election, the financial crisis arose generating the first bailout bill. McCain's first mistake was his initial panic suspending his campaign (9.4.2 Panic Defense). He could have easily defended himself against Obama's attacks based on the financial crisis had he used the trends in his favor and changed the momentum of the campaign. What would he have had to do?

1. During a crisis, we must know which way the trend is going. McCain failed to recognize that the public, Republican, independent, and Democrat, were all against the bailout. This was largely because he listened only to those inside of the beltway.

2. During a crisis, we must make a judgment about how long the trend will last. With the election so close, it should have been obvious that this was going to be the deciding issue of the campaign. Indeed, discussing any other issue during the crisis was a waste of air.

3. During a crisis, we must know where opponents stand. Obama took a clear stand in favor of the bailout. This stand was supported mostly by the Democrats in Congress, with the Republican legislators, despite President Bush's support, largely opposed.

4. *During a crisis, we must angle into a position that puts the trend behind us and against our opponents.* McCain should have taken a clear position against the bailouts, with the trend of public opinion. He should have used it to position himself against big government supporting big corporations with big spending. He should have also used it as a clear opportunity to break with President Bush's fiscal policy saving himself from the guilt-from-association charges of Obama (9.4.4 Defending Alliances). Would this have provided a tipping point in the election? Like Kerry's failure to use decent strategy against Bush in 2004, we will never know.

9.5.0 Crisis Exploitation

Sun Tzu's five key methods about how to successfully use an opponent's crisis.

"When you use fire to assist your attacks, you are clever."

Sun Tzu's The Art of War 12:3:1

"Rhythm is the basis of life, not steady forward progress. The forces of creation, destruction, and preservation have a whirling, dynamic interaction."

Kabbalah

General Principle:

We must use environment vulnerabilities against opponents only when it advances *our* position.

Situation:

While our primary concern is defending our position during a crisis, we cannot overlook opportunities to use a crisis against rivals, but sparking a crisis to attack an opponent is very dangerous. The firestorms that we spark are unpredictable and can easily blow back on us. One of the most common and easily avoidable mistakes in competitive strategy is to focus on hurting competitors rather than on advancing our own position. If these attacks weaken our position while destroying a competitor, it is just a matter of time until a new competitor arises to attack our weakened position. No matter how many competitors we destroy, we will always have new competitors arise to take their place (1.3.1 Competitive Comparison).

Opportunity:

Exploiting a crisis is most valuable in fixed sum competitions where we can only advance our position at our competitor's expense (7.6 Productive Competition). It works best when it is used productively, to create partnerships and alliances with former enemies. When either undermining opponents, sparking a crisis is like a loophole in the rule about conflict being too costly (3.1.3 Conflict Cost). The environment does the damage to our opponents, and we simply take advantage of it. The question is really whether or not sparking a crisis for competitors really helps us. This is not a question of altruism but of rational selfinterest.

Key Methods:

The five key methods for using a crisis simply reverse the methods for defense against a firestorm (3.2.5 Dynamic Reversal).

1. To spark a crisis against opponents, we wait for enough fuel in the environment. It takes time for fuel to build up. We cannot create this fuel. It must build up in the environment in sufficient quantities that we can use it to create a real crisis. We must simply recognize how it can be used against an opposing position (9.1 Climate Vulnerability).

2. To spark a crisis against opponents, we must know where our opponents are vulnerable to a crisis. This determines where we want to damage our opponent's resources: individual people, liquid resources, transportation and communication, long-term assets, or organizational reputation. (9.2 Points of Vulnerability).

3. To spark a crisis against opponents, we need a safe method to utilize the crisis. This is the most difficult step because each of the five methods for using crisis against an opponents can hurt us if we do not execute them correctly (9.4 Crisis Defense).

4. To spark a crisis against opponents, we need a clear, long-term benefit creating the crisis. This benefit can be an alliance as well as hurting the competitor. Because the risks are certain and the decision irrevocable, the benefit must even be more certain than our usual high standards for exploring opportunities (9.5.1 Adversarial Opportunities).

5. To spark a crisis against opponents, we must act on rational self-interest not on emotion. Emotions are temporary and we will almost certainly feel different in the future (9.5.2 Avoiding Emotion).

Illustration:

A negative example of how these principles were violated is provided by the Kerry campaign against Bush in the 2004 US presidential election. In that campaign, Kerry ran primarily on attacking Bush for going to war in Iraq.

1. To spark a crisis against opponents, we wait for enough fuel in the environment. In 2004, there wasn't enough war weariness among the general public and there wouldn't be until the 2006 Congressional elections when issues of corruption and government spending were added to the mix.

2. To spark a crisis against opponents, we must know where our opponents are vulnerable to a crisis. Kerry choose to make these attacks personal, portray Bush simultaneously as a fool for thinking there were WMDs in Iraq and an evil genius for convincing the world of it. This was a difficult target because people don't want to think of their president in a bad ***personal*** light, even when they may not want him to continue as president. A better target would have been the organization, the Republican Party.

3. To spark a crisis against opponents, we need a safe method to utilize the crisis. Because Kerry launched his attack too directly, one of the primary issues of the campaign became Kerry's flip-flops on the war. "He was for it before he was against it," is one of the more memorable lines from the campaign because of this miscalculation. A less overt method of using the situation was required.

4. To spark a crisis against opponents, we need a clear, long-term benefit creating the crisis. Because elections are a fixed-sum game, there is always a clear benefit. Here, the question is about a long-term one. Kerry left himself in no position to come back from a very close loss because of this miscalculation. He positioned himself solely an anti-Bush candidate and Bush wasn't running again.

5. To spark a crisis against opponents, we must act on rational self-interest not on emotion. Kerry could have won easily if he had based his campaign on retiring President Bush with honor because his time had passed rather than attacking him. Kerry could have made a strong argument that Bush's decisions on war, right or wrong, had changed the situation so that we needed a different type of leadership. However, the anger on the left against Bush required turning the election into an attack rather than a success.

9.5.1 Adversarial Opportunities

Sun Tzu's eight key methods on how our opponents' crises can create opportunities.

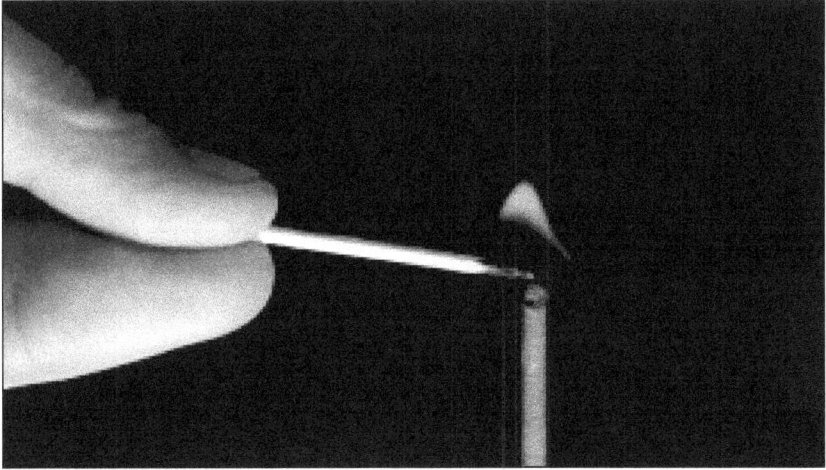

"Never waste an opportunity to defeat your enemy."
Sun Tzu's The Art of War 4:3:25

"An opponent is entitled to the same regard for his principles as we would expect others to have for ours. Non-violence demands that we should seek every opportunity to win over opponents."
Mohandas Gandhi

General Principle:

We must use a crisis against opponents when it strengthens our position.

Situation:

Our success depends on making the moves that improve our position. We must never undertake an action simply to create problems for competitors, but we must always make problems for our competition when it profits our position to do so. If there is no advantage using a crisis against our competitors, we cannot let the pressure of events seduce us into acting against them. If there is a advantage, however, we cannot ignore the opportunity out of some misplaced sense of benevolence. While we may actively work to spark a crisis, it comes from the environment. If we don't take advantage of the situation, another competitor is likely to. We can destroy our own position by fighting our opponents, but we can also destroy our position by not using every reasonable opportunity to advance it.

Opportunity:

Expanding into undefended areas is the usual basis for improving our position because it allows us to control resource while avoiding costly conflict (3.1.2 Strategic Profitability). Sun Tzu's method is to develop positions that others want to join rather than fight. A crisis can aid us in both directions: getting opponents to join us or opening opposing positions to attack. Getting resources from competitors weakens them while strengthening our position (3.5 Strength and Weakness). A victory over a once dominating competitor can dramatically change our momentum (7.0 Creating Momentum). Because most people judge competition in terms of winners and losers, a visible victory over a competitor changes people's opinions more than more subtle advances in position (1.2 Subobjective Positions).

Key Methods:

Using a crisis must meet a similar cost/benefits analysis that we use in choosing opportunities and actions. There are eight key methods we use.

1. We act only if using the crisis is likely to return more over the long term than it costs. The crisis decreases our costs, but it may also decrease our potential benefits (3.1 Strategic Economics.

2. We act only if we have the excess resources needed to trigger the crisis. Especially during a crisis, we cannot risk resources needed for production or defense (3.3 Opportunity Resources).

3. We act only if the nature of the crisis is likely to make us stronger and our opponents weaker. This means understanding the objective nature of the crisis and the nature of our relative strengths and weaknesses (3.5 Strength and Weakness).

4. We act only if the nature of the ground and the distance between us favors our move. If we don't understand the nature of the ground, we are always better passing the opportunity (4.3 Leveraging Form , 4.4 Strategic Distance , 4.5 Opportunity Surfaces).

5. We act only if the general climate supports our move. We cannot fight the general trends in the competitive arena even if we can ally or defeat a competitor (4.8 Climate Support).

6. We act only to serve our mission rather than acting under the pressure of events. This is especially a problem under the pressure of a crisis because it is so time sensitive (5.1 Mission Priorities , 5.1.1 Event Pressure).

7. We act only if we can complete our move before the crisis passes. Again, because of the temporary nature of a crisis, this window of opportunity is smaller than usual (5.3 Reaction Time).

8. We act only if we can use the crisis with a small, focused surgical strike. The whole purpose of using a crisis is to minimize our direct involvement. If we have to undertake a major program, this doesn't make sense (5.5 Focused Power5.4 Minimizing Action).

Illustration:

For our illustration, let us discuss Goldman Sachs's use of the financial crisis of 2008-2010 because it demonstrates both the value and dangers of an environmental crisis.

1. We act only if using the crisis is likely to return more over the long term than it costs. In 200607, Goldman was issuing subprime-mortgage securities (CDOs) to investors. At the same time, shorting the subprime-mortgage market through credit default swaps (CDS). This means that it made money selling the securities at the time, and, over the longer-term, it would make money if those investments turned bad. This gave them an incentive to expose the problems with subprime investments, at least secretly.

2. We act only if we have the excess resources needed to trigger the crisis. As always, the fuel was provided by the environment, We are not going to speculate on what resources, if any, Goldman use to spark the crisis. In February, 2007, The Federal Home Loan Mortgage Corporation (Freddie Mac) announced that it will no longer buy the most risky subprime mortgages and related securities. By June, Standard and Poor's and Moody's rating services downgraded over 100 subprime mortgages bonds. Goldman's biggest rival, Bear Stearns, had to liquidate two hedge funds of mortgage-backed securities.

3. We act only if the nature of the crisis is likely to make us stronger and our opponents weaker. When the market collapsed, Goldman made a huge trading profit - including about $13 billion provided by U.S. taxpayers as part of the AIG bailout. These profits became the basis for an SEC fraud lawsuit, but not until 2010.

4. We act only if the nature of the ground and the distance between us favors our move. The head of the Treasury determines how the government acts in addressing financial markets. Robert Rubin, Clinton's Treasury Secretary, spent 26 years at Goldman. Bush's Treasury Secretary Paulson was Goldman CEO for 25 years. Obama's Treasury Secretary is Tim Geithner, chose Mark Patterson, an ex-lobbyist from Goldman Sachs, to be his chief of staff. Among his chief advisors are several Goldman executives, including John Thain, Goldman's former co-president. Neel Kashkari, who heads the $700 billion TARP bailout, was vice president at Goldman. Paulson put Goldman vicechairman, Ed Liddy, as CEO of AIG.

5. We act only if the general climate supports our move. Goldman's network of industry and political connections shaped the way government has responded to the economic crisis. Merrill CEO John Thain's Goldman credibility caused Secretary Paulson and Geithner to help the quick sale of Merrill to Bank of America and, on the same weekend let Lehman Brothers, which did not have Goldman's strong connections in Washington, fail. Some claim that Paulson and Geithner permitted Lehman to fail in order to eliminate a significant Goldman competitor. Paulson and Geithner were kinder to AIG, who insured Goldman's investments through credit swaps. They gave AIG an $85 billion loan, later increased to $123 billion, to prevent the insurance giant from failing.

6. *We act only to serve our mission rather than acting under the pressure of events.* Getting more than $23 billion in direct and indirect federal aid, Goldman initially emerged intact from the crisis, limiting its subprime losses to $1.5 billion. By repaying $10 billion in direct federal bailouts, it escaped tough federal limits on 2009 executives' bonuses. Goldman announced record earnings in July, and surpassed $50 billion in revenue in 2009, paying its employees more than $20 billion in year-end bonuses.

7. *We act only if we can complete our move before the crisis passes.* At the beginning of 2007, there were five investment banks. Afterward, Lehman Brothers was in bankruptcy and two others, Merrill Lynch, and Bear Stearns were acquired by other companies with their stockholders as the big losers. Two companies survived, Morgan Stanley and Goldman Sachs. Both were allowed to change their stature from from an investment bank to bank holding company to eliminate much of their regulatory burdens.

8. *We act only if we can use the crisis with a small, focused surgical strike.* This is where Goldman Sachs ran into problems because the crisis and its fallout continues. The current SEC suit for fraud is serious, but not life-threatening. However, the SEC discovery process will enable government lawyers to search Goldman's records, quite potentially raising Goldman's liabilities. This lawsuit could end up breaking up Goldman Sachs.

9.5.2 Avoiding Emotion

Sun Tzu's six key methods on the danger of exploiting environmental vulnerabilities for purely emotion reasons.

"As leader, you cannot let your anger interfere with the success of your forces.
As commander, you cannot let yourself become enraged before you go to battle."

Sun Tzu's The Art of War 12:4:10-12

"To be angry about trifles is mean and childish; to rage and be furious is brutish; and to maintain perpetual wrath is akin to the practice and temper of devils; but

to prevent and suppress rising resentment is wise and glorious, is manly and divine."

Alan Watts

General Principle:

We must never trigger a crisis for opponents on the basis of emotions.

Situation:

Negative emotions such as anger and hatred are true enemies of strategic decision-making. Emotion is good for creating action but bad for making decisions. Such emotions transform opponents into villains. Villains must be stopped at any cost but Sun Tzu's strategy requires balancing costs and benefits, risks and rewards. During a crisis, over-reaction is the real danger, and strong emotions encourage overreaction. Emotions arise naturally from competitive situations because we care about our mission and our values. By definition, adversaries oppose those values. The problem is that seeking to hurt others takes us away from our goal of advancing our position. Wars of attrition are the opposite of developing positions that others want to join rather than oppose.

Opportunity:

Ignorance about the future creates fear, but we must accept our ignorance to see opportunities (2.3.2 Reaction Unpredictability). Seemingly unpleasant events can open paths that lead to great things. Sun Tzu's strategy is a method of adapting because what goes "wrong" can be a fertile source of opportunities (3.2.5 Dynamic Reversal). Our adversaries are rivals because they are like us. Someone with whom we are competing today can be our ally tomorrow. We may portray our enemies as absolute evil to unite and rally our supporters, but we cannot afford to make our decisions about opponents based on emotion (1.1.1 Position Dynamics).

Key Methods:

These key methods help us avoid emotional decisions that are all too common crisis.

*1. **We must reserve our emotions for caring about our mission*** and our people. Caring creates strength and unity. We work to serve our mission so we should not get upset because others work for their mission. The best solution is always finding a way to bring our missions together (1.6.1 Shared Mission).

*2. **We must focus on positions not personalities.*** Personalities can rub us the wrong way, but it is harder to get angry when we think conceptually about positions. When we automatically think in terms of positions, it takes personal conflict out of our analysis (3.2.5 Dynamic Reversal).

*3. **We must see opposing positions from an outside, not opposing, perspective**.* We develop broad contact networks so that we don't miss vital elements from our own point of view (2.0 Developing Perspective).

*4. **We must remember that we must make each move pay**.* Emotions of hostility tempt us into expensive conflicts and can create feuds which lead to more conflict in the future (3.1.3 Conflict Cost).

*5. **We must respond to the situation, not to the emotion it creates**.* Learning to recognize situations is a powerful prescription for controlling emotion since it channels our energy into instant reaction. The complex array of conditions should engage our mind to such a degree that we don't have time for emotions (5.1.1 Event Pressure , 6.0 Situation Response).

*6. **We must think in terms of the big picture and long-term rather than the local moment**.* Our positions last. Our emotions don't. Because of this, we cannot let our temporary emotions hurt our position (1.1 Position Paths).

Illustration:

Let's apply these principles to the strategic problem of deciding whether or not to get even with a co-worker. This is from an actual case from a Science of Strategy Institute member, let's call him John. After a meeting where a coworker, let us call her Jane, stabbed him in the back, John found himself consumed with plotting revenge. We must reserve our emotion for caring about our mission and our people. After thinking about it, John realized that Jane was a pure distractions from his goals within the organization and that hurting her couldn't get him any closer to those goals.

1. We must focus on positions not personalities. Though he found Jane a detestable person, her position on the organization really had no affect on his own, neither obstructing him or competing with him.

2. We must see opposing positions from an outside, not opposing, perspective. John realized that from the perspective of the people who matter, his bosses and customers, a vendetta against Jane could only make him look bad.

3. We must remember that we must make each move pay. John realized that in thinking about Jane, he was wasting valuable time he should be spending on his project.

4. We must respond to the situation, not to the emotion it creates. Though the problem during the meeting was personally insulting, no one realized it but him so there was no real problem that needed to be addressed.

5. We must think in terms of the big picture and long-term rather than the local moment. John decided to forget about Jane, to avoid dealing with her in the future if he could, but generally put the event behind him.

9.6.0 Constant Vigilance

Sun Tzu's five key methods describing where to focus our attention to preserve our positions.

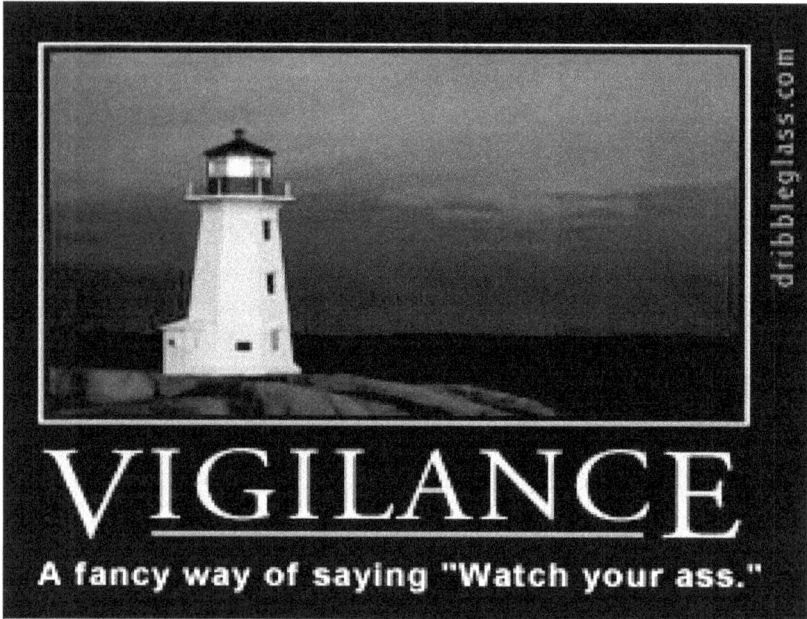

VIGILANCE
A fancy way of saying "Watch your ass."

"You can watch and guard for years.
Then a single battle can determine victory in a day."
Sun Tzu's The Art of War 13:1:10-11

"Eternal vigilance is the price of liberty."
John Philpot Curran

General Principle:

We must use constant vigilance to defend our position.

Situation:

Constant vigilance sounds good, but it presents a real challenge. Though the world is constantly changing, we are often blind to change. We offer an exercise in our live training that demonstrates how difficult to see what has changed in a static picture much less a complex situation (3.0 Identifying Opportunities). Since we miss so many of the critical changes taking place around us, facing the dynamics of change requires courage. Since the unknown creates fear, we are often in denial about the changes taking place around us. This is especially important regarding our vulnerabilities. Positions naturally decay over time. As positions get older, they become more and more vulnerable.

Opportunity:

While we don't know what the future will bring, change creates opportunities as well as vulnerabilities. Much of the same vigilance that allows us to identify our vulnerabilities also allows us to see our opportunities (3.0 Identifying Opportunities). If we see our vulnerabilities before a crisis, our existing position is always easy to defend. Though positions are constantly changing, these changes are not random. Our positions follow a certain path anchored in the past while moving into the future. Both opportunities and vulnerabilities are difficult to see by their nature (3.2.2 Opportunity Invisibility). The direction of our position is much easier to see if we continually compare it to the past using the right yardsticks.

Key Methods:

Vigilance, like all of Sun Tzu's strategy, is an adaptive loop (1.8.2 The Adaptive Loop). The following five key methods define its most valuable components.

1. We must continually re-examine each of the five elements that define our position. We do this normally in comparing our position with alternative positions, but in the analysis we want to look at what has changed in our current positions (1.3 Elemental Analysis).

*2. **We must continually re-evaluate our changing balance of strengths and weaknesses**.* Even improvements in our position in any given area can generate weaknesses (3.5 Strength and Weakness).

*3. **We must continually gauge the accumulation of fuel for a crisis in the environment**.* Strangely enough, our success itself can create fuel in the environment that can be used to fuel a crisis (9.1 Climate Vulnerability).

*4. **We must continually check the susceptibility of our five points of vulnerability**.* Our changing strengths and the accumulation of fuel threatens some areas more than others (9.2 Points of Vulnerability).

*5. **We must continually adjust our allocation of resources to shore up any points of vulnerability**.* As a defense, these adjustments are usually much less significant than moves used to pursue opportunities (6.0 Situation Response).

Illustration:

The aging of our bodies is a great demonstration of this principle. As we get older, our defenses break down. We can maintain our health only by more and more constant vigilance. As someone who is now in his late fifties and has already survived a fairly scary bout with cancer, I find that I am becoming more vigilant about defending my health. Applying the principles above to a health strategy:

*1. **We must continually re-examine each of the five elements that define our position**.* This means having a health mission, recognizing what drives changes and our limited control over our body, taking responsibility for our decisions, and having good healthy methods.

*2. **We must continually re-evaluate our changing balance of strengths and weaknesses**.* These changes in our health are driven both by time, events beyond our control, and our decisions.

3. We must continually gauge the accumulation of fuel for a crisis in the environment. Fuel for a crisis ranges from body fat to unhealthy habits. Our success in other areas in life can lead directly to less exercise and a worse diet.

4. We must continually check the susceptibility of our five points of vulnerability. While we might think that the only target is physical body, but key people (our doctors), our immediate resources (health insurance), communication and transportation (local accessibility to health care providers), our long-term assets (physical strength, good habits), and organization (our network of regular health care providers) are also important. As we age, it is especially important to have developed a reliable network of health care providers that we can access quickly should a problem arise. We cannot afford to trust to luck.

5. We must continually adjust our allocation of resources to shore up any points of vulnerability. Getting more disciplined about exercise, cutting down on drinking, and so on.

Glossary of Key Concepts from Sun Tzu's *The Art of War*

This glossary is keyed to the most common English words used in the translation of *The Art of War*. Those terms only capture the strategic concepts generally. Though translated as English nouns, verbs, adverbs, or adjectives, the Chinese characters on which they are based are totally conceptual, not parts of speech. For example, the character for conflict is translated as the noun "conflict," as the verb "fight," and as the adjective "disputed." Ancient written Chinese was a conceptual language, not a spoken one. More like mathematical terms, these concepts are primarily defined by the strict structure of their relationships with other concepts. The Chinese names shown in parentheses with the characters are primarily based on Pinyin, but we occasionally use Cantonese terms to make each term unique.

Advance (*Jeun* 進): to move into new **ground**; to expand your **position**; to move forward in a campaign; the opposite of **flee**.

Advantage, *benefit* (*Li* 利)**:** an opportunity arising from having a better **position** relative to an **enemy**; an opening left by an **enemy**; a **strength** that matches against an **enemy's weakness**; where fullness meets emptiness; a desirable characteristic of a strategic **position**.

Aim, *vision, foresee* (*Jian* 見)**: focus** on a specific **advantage**, opening, or opportunity; predicting movements of an **enemy**; a skill of a **leader** in observing **climate**.

Analysis, *plan* (*Gai* 計): a comparison of relative **position**; the examination of the five factors that define a strategic **position**; a combination of **knowledge** and **vision**; the ability to see through **deception**.

Army: see **war.**

Attack, *invade* (*Gong* 攻): a movement to new **ground**; advancing a strategic **position**; action against an **enemy** in the sense of moving into his **ground**; opposite of **defend**; does not necessarily mean **conflict**.

Bad, *ruined* (*Pi* 圯): a condition of the **ground** that makes **advance** difficult; destroyed; terrain that is broken and difficult to traverse; one of the nine situations or types of terrain.

Barricaded: see **obstacles.**

Battle (*Zhan* 戰): to challenge; to engage an **enemy;** generically, to meet a challenge; to choose a confrontation with an **enemy** at a specific time and place; to focus all your resources on a task; to establish superiority in a **position**; to challenge an **enemy** to increase **chaos;** that which is **controlled** by **surprise;** one of the four forms of **attack;** the response to a **desperate situation;** character meaning was originally "big meeting," though later took on the meaning "big weapon"; not necessarily **conflict.**

Bravery, *courage* (*Yong* 勇): the ability to face difficult choices; the character quality that deals with the changes of **CLIMATE;** courage of conviction; willingness to act on vision; one of the six characteristics of a leader.

Break, *broken, divided* (*Po* 破): to **divide** what is **complete**; the absence of a **uniting philosophy**; the opposite of unity.

Calculate, *count* (*Shu* 数): mathematical comparison of quantities and qualities; a measurement of **distance** or troop size.

Change, *transform* (*Bian* 變): transition from one **condition** to another; the ability to adapt to different situations; a natural characteristic of **climate**.

Chaos, *disorder* (*Juan* 亂): **conditions** that cannot be **foreseen**; the natural state of confusion arising from **battle**; one of six weaknesses of an organization; the opposite of **control**.

Claim, *position, form* (*Xing* 形): to use the **ground**; a shape or specific condition of **ground**; the **ground** that you **control**; to use the benefits of the **ground**; the formations of troops; one of the four key skills in making progress.

Climate, *heaven* (*Tian* 天): the passage of time; the realm of uncontrollable **change**; divine providence; the weather; trends that **change** over time; generally, the future; what one must **aim** at in the future; one of five key factors in **analysis;** the opposite of **ground**.

Command (*Ling* 令): to order or the act of ordering subordinates; the decisions of a **leader**; the creation of **methods**.

Competition: see *war.*

Complete: see *unity.*

Condition: see **ground.**

Confined, *surround* (*Wei* 圍): to encircle; a **situation** or **stage** in which your options are limited; the proper tactic for dealing with an **enemy** that is ten times smaller; to seal off a smaller **enemy**; the characteristic of a **stage** in which a larger **force** can be attacked by a smaller one; one of nine **situations** or **stages**.

Conflict, *fight* (*Zheng* 爭): to contend; to dispute; direct confrontation of arms with an **enemy**; highly desirable **ground** that creates disputes; one of nine types of **ground,** terrain, or stages.

Constricted, *narrow* (*Ai* 狹): a confined space or niche; one of six field positions; the limited extreme of the dimension distance; the opposite of **spread-out.**

Control, *govern* (*Chi* 治): to manage situations; to overcome disorder; the opposite of **chaos.**

Dangerous: see **serious.**

Dangers, *adverse* (Ak 阨): a condition that makes it difficult to **advance**; one of three dimensions used to evaluate advantages; the dimension with the extreme field **positions** of **entangling** and **supporting**.

Death, *desperate* (*Si* 死): to end or the end of life or efforts; an extreme situation in which the only option is **battle**; one of nine **stages** or types of **terrain**; one of five types of **spies**; opposite of **survive**.

Deception, *bluffing, illusion* (*Gui* 詭):
to control perceptions; to control information; to mislead an **enemy**; an attack on an opponent's **aim**; the characteristic of war that confuses perceptions.

Defend (*Shou* 守): to guard or to hold a **ground**; to remain in a **position**; the opposite of **attack**.

Detour (*Yu* 迂): the indirect or unsuspected path to a **position**; the more difficult path to **advantage**; the route that is not **direct**.

Direct, *straight* (*Jik* 直): a straight or obvious path to a goal; opposite of **detour**.

Distance, *distant* (*Yuan* 遠): the space separating **ground**; to be remote from the current location; to occupy **positions** that are not close to one another; one of six field positions; one of the three dimensions for evaluating opportunities; the emptiness of space.

Divide, *separate* (*Fen* 分): to break apart a larger force; to separate from a larger group; the opposite of **join** and **focus**.

Double agent, *reverse* (*Fan* 反): to turn around in direction; to change a situation; to switch a person's allegiance; one of five types of spies.

Easy, *light* (*Qing* 輕): to require little effort; a **situation** that requires little effort; one of nine **stages** or types of terrain; opposite of **serious**.

Emotion, *feeling* (*Xin* 心): an unthinking reaction to **aim**, a necessary element to inspire **moves**; a component of esprit de corps; never a sufficient cause for **attack**.

Enemy, *competitor* (*Dik* 敵): one who makes the same **claim**; one with a similar **goal**; one with whom comparisons of capabilities are made.

Entangling, *hanging* (*Gua* 懸): a **position** that cannot be returned to; any **condition** that leaves no easy place to go; one of six field positions.

Evade, *avoid* (*Bi* 避): the tactic used by small competitors when facing large opponents.

Fall apart, *collapse* (*Beng* 崩): to fail to execute good decisions; to fail to use a **constricted position**; one of six weaknesses of an organization.

Fall down, *sink* (*Haam* 陷): to fail to make good decisions; to **move** from a **supporting position**; one of six weaknesses of organizations.

Feelings, *affection, love* (*Ching* 情): the bonds of relationship; the result of a shared **philosophy**; requires management.

Fight, *struggle* (Dou 鬥): to engage in **conflict**; to face difficulties.

Fire (*Huo* 火): an environmental weapon; a universal analogy for all weapons.

Flee, *retreat, northward* (*Bei* 北) :to abandon a **position**; to surrender **ground**; one of six weaknesses of an **army**; opposite of **advance**.

Focus, *concentrate* (*Zhuan* 專): to bring resources together at a given time; to **unite** forces for a purpose; an attribute of having a shared **philosophy**; the opposite of *divide*.

Force (*Lei* 力): power in the simplest sense; a **group** of people bound by **unity** and **focus**; the relative balance of **strength** in opposition to **weakness**.

Foresee: see **aim**.

Fullness: see **strength**.

General: see **leader**.

Goal: see **philosophy**.

Ground, *situation, stage* (*Di* 地): the earth; a specific place; a specific condition; the place one competes; the prize of competition; one of five key factors in competitive analysis; the opposite of **climate**.

Groups, *troops* (*Dui* 隊): a number of people united under a shared **philosophy**; human resources of an organization; one of the five targets of fire attacks.

Inside, *internal* (*Nei* 內): within a **territory** or organization; an insider; one of five types of spies; opposite of *Wai*, outside.

Intersecting, *highway* (*Qu* 衢): a **situation** or **ground** that allows you to **join**; one of nine types of terrain.

Join (*Hap* 合): to unite; to make allies; to create a larger **force**; opposite of **divide**.

Knowledge, *listening* (*Zhi*: 知): to have information; the result of listening; the first step in advancing a **position**; the basis of strategy.

Lax, *loosen* (*Shii* 弛): too easygoing; lacking discipline; one of six weaknesses of an army.

Leader, *general, commander* (*Jiang* 將):
the decision-maker in a competitive unit; one who **listens** and **aims**; one who manages **troops**; superior of officers and men; one of the five key factors in analysis; the conceptual opposite of fa, the established methods, which do not require decisions.

Learn, *compare* (*Xiao* 效): to evaluate the relative qualities of **enemies**.

Listen, *obey* (*Ting* 聽): to gather **knowledge**; part of **analysis**.

Listening: see **knowledge**.

Local, *countryside* (_Xiang_ 鄉): the nearby **ground**; to have **knowledge** of a specific **ground**; one of five types of **spies**.

Marsh (_Ze_ 澤): **ground** where footing is unstable; one of the four types of **ground**; analogy for uncertain situations.

Method: see **system**.

Mission: see **philosophy**.

Momentum, *influence* (_Shi_ 勢): the **force** created by **surprise** set up by **standards;** used with **timing**.

Mountains, *hill, peak* (_Shan_ 山): uneven **ground**; one of four types of **ground**; an analogy for all unequal **situations**.

Move, *march, act* (_Hang_ 行): action toward a position or goal; used as a near synonym for _dong_, act.

Nation (_Guo_ 國): the state; the productive part of an organization; the seat of political power; the entity that controls an **army** or competitive part of the organization.

Obstacles, *barricaded* (_Xian_ 險): to have barriers; one of the three characteristics of the **ground**; one of six field positions; as a field position, opposite of **unobstructed**.

Open, *meeting, crossing* (_Jiao_ 來): to share the same **ground** without conflict; to come together; a **situation** that encourages a race; one of nine **terrains** or **stages**.

Opportunity: see _advantage._

Outmaneuver (_Sou_ 走): to go astray; to be **forced** into a **weak position**; one of six weaknesses of an army.

Outside, *external* (_Wai_ 外): not within a **territory** or **army**; one who has a different perspective; one who offers an objective view; opposite of **internal**.

Philosophy, *mission, goals* (_Tao_ 道): the shared **goals** that **unite** an **army**; a system of thought; a shared viewpoint; literally "the way"; a way to work together; one of the five key factors in **analysis**.

Plateau (_Liu_ 陸): a type of **ground** without defects; an analogy for any equal, solid, and certain **situation**; the best place for competition; one of the four types of **ground**.

Resources, *provisions* (_Liang_ 糧): necessary supplies, most commonly food; one of the five targets of fire attacks.

Restraint: see **timing.**

Reward, *treasure, money* (*Bao* 賞): profit; wealth; the necessary compensation for competition; a necessary ingredient for **victory**; **victory** must pay.

Scatter, *dissipating* (*San* 散): to disperse; to lose **unity**; the pursuit of separate **goals** as opposed to a central **mission**; a situation that causes a **force** to scatter; one of nine conditions or types of terrain.

Serious, *heavy* (*Chong* 重): any task requiring effort and skill; a **situation** where resources are running low when you are deeply committed to a campaign or heavily invested in a project; a situation where opposition within an organization mounts; one of nine **stages** or types of **terrain.**

Siege (*Gong Cheng* 攻城): to move against entrenched positions; any movement against an **enemy's strength**; literally "strike city"; one of the four forms of attack; the least desirable form of attack.

Situation: see **ground.**

Speed, *hurry* (Sai 馳): to **move** over **ground** quickly; the ability to **advance positions** in a minimum of time; needed to take advantage of a window of opportunity.

Spread-out, *wide* (*Guang* 廣): a surplus of **distance**; one of the six **ground positions**; opposite of **constricted.**

Spy, *conduit, go-between* (*Gaan* 間): a source of information; a channel of communication; literally, an "opening between."

Stage: see **ground.**

Standard, *proper, correct* (*Jang* 正): the expected behavior; the standard approach; proven methods; the opposite of surprise; together with **surprise** creates **momentum.**

Storehouse, *house* (*Ku* 庫): a place where resources are stockpiled; one of the five targets for fire attacks.

Stores, *accumulate, savings* (*Ji* 糧): resources that have been stored; any type of inventory; one of the five targets of fire attacks.

Strength, *fullness, satisfaction* (*Sat* 壹): wealth or abundance or resources; the state of being crowded; the opposite of Xu, empty.

Supply wagons, *transport* (*Zi* 輜): the movement of **resources** through **distance**; one of the five targets of fire attacks.

Support, *supporting* (*Zhii* 支): to prop up; to enhance; a **ground position** that you cannot leave without losing **strength**; one of six field positions; the opposite extreme of gua, entangling.

Surprise, *unusual, strange* (*Qi* 奇) : the unexpected; the innovative; the opposite of **standard**; together with **standards** creates **momentum**.

Surround: see **confined**.

Survive, *live, birth* (*Shaang* 生): the state of being created, started, or beginning; the state of living or surviving; a temporary condition of fullness; one of five types of spies; the opposite of **death**.

System, *method* (*Fa* 法): a set of procedures; a group of techniques; steps to accomplish a **goal**; one of the five key factors in analysis; the realm of groups who must follow procedures; the opposite of the **leader**.

Territory, *terrain*: see **ground**.

Timing, *restraint* (*Jie* 節): to withhold action until the proper time; to release tension; a companion concept to **momentum**.

Troops: see **group**.

Unity, *whole, oneness* (*Yi* 一): the characteristic of a **group** that shares a **philosophy**; the lowest number; a **group** that acts as a unit; the opposite of **divided**.

Unobstructed, *expert* (*Tong* 通): without obstacles or barriers; **ground** that allows easy movement; open to new ideas; one of six field positions; opposite of **obstructed**.

Victory, *win, winning* (*Sing* 勝): success in an endeavor; getting a reward; serving your mission; an event that produces more than it consumes; to make a profit.

War, *competition, army* (**Bing** 兵): a dynamic situation in which **positions** can be won or lost; a contest in which a **reward** can be won; the conditions under which the principles of strategy work.

Water, *river* (*Shui* 水): a fast-changing **ground**; fluid **conditions**; one of four types of **ground**; an analogy for change.

Weakness, *emptiness, need* (*Xu* 虛): the absence of people or resources; devoid of **force**; the point of **attack** for an **advantage**; a characteristic of **ground** that enables **speed**; poor; the opposite of strength.

Win, *winning*: see **victory**.

Wind, *fashion, custom* (*Feng* 風): the pressure of environmental forces.

The *Art of War Playbook* Series

There are over two-hundred and thirty articles on Sun Tzu's competitive principles in the nine volumes of the *Art of War Playbook*. Each volume covers a specific area of Sun Tzu strategy.

VOLUME ONE: - POSITIONS

VOLUME TWO: -PERSPECTIVE

VOLUME THREE: - OPPORTUNITIES

VOLUME FOUR: - PROBABILITY

VOLUME FIVE: - MISTAKES

VOLUME SIX: - SITUATIONS

VOLUME SEVEN: - MOMENTUM

VOLUME EIGHT: - REWARDS

VOLUME NINE: - VULNERABILITIES.

About the Translator and Author

Gary Gagliardi is recognized as America's leading expert on Sun Tzu's *The Art of War*. An award-winning author and business strategist, his many books on Sun Tzu's strategy have been translated around the world. He has appeared on hundreds of talk shows nationwide, providing strategic insight on the breaking news. He has trained decision makers from some of the world's most successful organizations in competitive thinking. His workshops convert Sun Tzu's many principles into a series of practical tools for handling common competitive challenges.

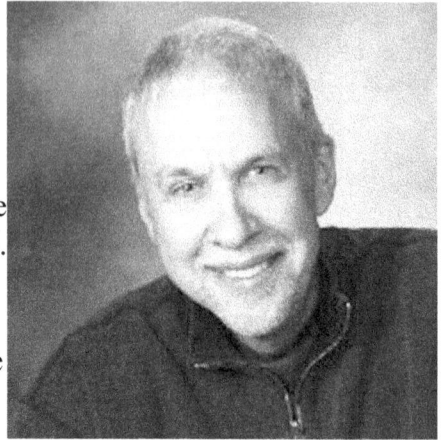

Gary began using Sun Tzu's competitive principles in a successful corporate career and when he started his own software company. In 1990, he wrote his first *Art of War* adaptation for his company's salespeople. By 1992, his company was on *Inc. Magazine's* list of the 500 fastest-growing privately held companies in America. He personally won the U.S. Chamber of Commerce Blue Chip Quality Award and was an Ernst and Young Entrepreneur of the Year finalist. His customers—AT&T, GE, and Motorola, among others—began inviting him to speak at their conferences. After becoming a multimillionaire when he sold his software company in 1997, he continued teaching *The Art of War* around the world.

Gary has authored several breakthrough works on *The Art of War*. Ten of his books on strategy have won book award recognition in nine different non-fiction categories.

Art of War Books by Gary Gagliardi

Gary Gagliardi's Books are Available at:

SunTzus.com
Amazon.com
BarnesAndNoble.com
Itunes.apple.com

www.ingramcontent.com/pod-product-compliance
Lightning Source LLC
Chambersburg PA
CBHW062029200326
41519CB00017B/4981